Vital Honor:

I0081349

Unlocking Erotic Memory

A NOVEL

GURU TARACHIMA

OM SHALOM PUBLISHING

"A guide to spiritual investigation, Vital Honor of the Sacred: Unlocking Erotic Memory , is an inspiration for all ages on a journey home, a personal revelation of deep insight and ancient wisdom."

" Guru Tara is a natural leader, an extraordinarily gifted writer, a radiant and beautiful woman, who brings an unusually sensitive understanding to being a healer in today's complex world."

" Guru Tarachi, brings a deep, heart wrenching, poetic sensitivity to her writing, a clarity and truth which one cannot look away from."

Forbidden

Loyalty,

Sacred Sacrifice

Natural tattoos,

Red Ochre, high priestess

Shaman scrolls

On her naked skin

Like the silkworm you have built a cocoon around

yourself. Who will save you?

Burst your own cocoon and come out as the Beautiful

butterfly, as

the free soul.

My real life was the fantasy before the reality set in. The real me, the one with the strawberry colored vintage glasses my grandmother wore, the ones that made my movie star appearance even stronger. She knew. How did she know how I walked the streets?

Everything I did was for God.

I wanted to be a doctor, a lawyer, anything to keep me off the streets. I would wander up and down Lexington Avenue at midnight, hoping someone would see me. Someone would notice my depth and inner beauty, I wore on the outside, inside of my catsuit. The black lace that adorned my body folded in layers around my skin, wove the portrait of a sacred intimate. The woman I had never wanted to become, yet was my isolation, in my desperation, I walked the streets in hopes of salvation.

Salvation from hunger, salvation from the wet nights, rain pouring down on my head. Soaking through my soul's light. I asked myself many times where home was, what family was, and where mine were ... there were no answers that came ... so I kept wandering, until someone saw through my veils and took down my walls...I had found home in the midst of war ... the inner peace that came in the midst of death and destruction was unbelievable, yet undeniable. The permeating sense of deep contradiction, paradox, embodied my mind's eye, although left no visible imprints on my body.

I was young and sexy, protected, or so I thought. I became a slave to the memories that haunted my soul. The memories that I did not know existed, until many years later.

The day he walked into the courtroom, all fell still, and I knew it to be true. The rape, the exorbitant amount of money he paid to have me followed, the lengths he went to betray my soul. A

Buddhist monk, would have compassion for his karma, his

destroyer tendency. Was I a victim or a survivor?

Part One

I woke up at night, in the middle of the rain forest in Mexico, high on Ayahuasca, journeying through the past as I moved through the world as a jaguar, my totem animal. My guide was an experienced shaman, in a far off land, which was much closer than I thought, to an inner world where the back realms of the spiritual world were so closely woven together.

There were many natural trips, without the use of drugs, and many experienced shamanic teachers. I decided very early on, that there was not going to be any intoxicants that lubricated my mind artificially, somewhere I knew that if I released the poisons into my body and mind they would not release me.

My own senses were my deeply spiritual roots hidden in the conch shells of addiction. He was the one, no he was the one, I saw every man as the potential for salvation. Who was the one who would save my soul, and body from destruction, from itself, from the memories I came to know.

Peace came with the knowing. The knowing came at night. The night became the welcoming greeting for work. Work became the night game of the starlit world of forgiveness and love. It was the time where I could be anyone I wanted to be, whatever name I chose for myself.

However, for whomever. I was never the same girl twice. I was a little girl lost in a big city, one that was being eaten by the weapons of mass destruction; guns that resembled penises, and the penises that resembled guns. The night that was lit by the moon, was welcomed by my body, who did not know it was on it's way to becoming awakened to the terror only it knew.

The memories, memories that came flooding back on that street corner in Nam. When he jumped out of the bushes and ran me into the floor with his cock. He came shooting through his only weapon left, and I, mine. My heart, my only weapon, begging him to stop, and wait until we could go to a nicer place, in a nicer way. I blacked out in the black night. The moon no longer shone, and I lost the light that had lit the way to the streets.

I was lost. Then, a little girl found. Lying there on the streets of desperation, I became a nun.

A Jewish one.

That was me, then.

To be in proximity with God, my father, mother, my relationship above all else. Spun in many different directions. In and out of control.

Fingers of white lace, Caress my black skin

Pushed up against, A broken mirror

Swaying to the side, Of gentle acceptance

Gazing toward the haze, Misty-eyed Female

Power

Sings of Loving, Longing voices of prayer

The birds sing to us, sweetly, Of how we suffer by

longing for a moment

That no longer exits.

I was a simple Jew, descending from a long line of Rabbis. I could not understand why there were asking, Is there a G-d, is there not? My connection and dedication, my relationship with god was all I had. I gave over my power to obligation. I was what it said I was, like it always was, in my home. He said I was an idiot, a whore, and so be it! The Torah told me what to be and how to dress, I succumbed at long last, to a father that was not my own, to a community, a family I desperately longed for. For belonging and union, for a husband to make me whole. That was what I wanted more than anything. To be whole, to fill up the hole within my heart.

Come… come, whoever you are,

Wanderer, Worshipper, lover of leaving,

It doesn't matter.

Ours is not a caravan of despair,

Come, even if you have broken your vows

A thousand times

Come, yet again, come, come.

Pouring out blood and many tears to stay in a

world that could not hold me, and I it, I lost my

power in a flash of lightning. A power I had lost so

long ago, as an only child, I grew up lonely.

They were all seated in a row, all ready to go,

dressed in their best, the finest stressed

    As the train moved from its tracks

    In my arms, I remember, the yes, of the pink one

    Fur all ruffled from being held, so many times

In security and fear the wide eyes bear gave me

the strength

To hold back the tears

Be silent

Sometimes, although I heard their cries at night,

how could I have let them, stationary, if not for me

I was their only hope, and they

Were mine.

I drew a picture of a house, inside of the window

was written "The House of G-d. I knew I was a

priestess then at age four, destined to take

people down the glowing rainbow road, to light

each others light, ignite another's fire, inspiring

others to be in the flow

To be in love.

I wanted to build my own house of god

My own sanctuary, the home I never had. I didn't

have the patience

I wasn't ready

Showing up, falling in and out of the sacred spaces…
opening to holy and wholeness.

Embracing the broken and fractured parts of ourselves as
holy and whole, the path of total acceptance.

All of our truth as holy, whole, honor and shame may be the
flip side of the same coin. Two sides of the same coin,
universal and particular, just parts of one whole.

All day I read wordless scriptures, all night I practice no-practice meditation.

On the riverbank, a bush warbler

Sings in the weeping willow

In the sleeping village, a dog bays at the moon

Nothing troubles the free flow of my feelings

How can this mind be passed on?"

In the beginning, letting go of all preconceptions and notions of what a "normal" life, the American dream, would look like, in hopes of a deeper intimacy with the divine. I jumped into my destiny, going and staying in the holy land, of Israel, leaving behind a full scholarship to Columbia University, for a maybe fellowship in Jerusalem. Searching for soul purpose in my early twenties was not the solo grand tour I had envisioned. There was no other choice to be made, I dove into the deep waters of vast oceans unknown, to meet and greet many deceptions and truths.

Maybe the choice was saving me from my own destruction. Maybe the choice was the only choice to stay alive.

Choice, journeying into the excavation of my own soul.

Truth lies on all lips. Just underneath the desire for endless stamps of approval, rests the truth of your inner voice. How does speaking your truth, and revealing yourself to your self, and others create freedom?

Freedom from shame…freedom to be alive

Part of my search lead towards an earthly union. As many brides before them, they had opportunity to bless the young women standing in front of them in a line awaiting their blessing to become betrothed, as the Divine Goddess was said to be hovering above some someone about to married. The girls in line were mostly longing to sit the brides place, next week, or the next month. The goal of the Jewish Orthodox world was to get married and join the status of adulthood.

The kallah, the Hebrew word for bride said to me,
 May all of your dreams come true
May you find him in the right time,
B'sha tova, the standard blessing.

I couldn't inhale her words

I felt the pure light of the shechinah, divine
feminine

Shining down upon her, yet something inside
wouldn't allow me get too close.

The spiritual union I longed for,

Transformed my bitterness into angst.

As I continued to abandon myself, in search

of my self in another, a man to give me the

love I could not give to myself

A LOVE I did not know

Even If I saw it.

In the Jewish tradition, Friday night is sacred for Hieros
Gamos, or sexual communion, where the Masculine and
Feminine Divine unite and become One. This is seen as a
Mitzvah, or good deed, where the marriage bed is seen as
holy, the holy of holies, or inner sanctum, parallel to the holy of
holies in the Temple of Jerusalem, where the high priest prayed

on the highest holy days, where Presence dwells. The idea of a purely masculine divinity is truly ludicrous as men themselves come into being through the womb of a woman. The model for creation is of and through a feminine and masculine divinity. The denial of a feminine deity is the denial of creation itself, and of the innate feminine inside each man, and the masculine inside of each woman. Both aspects must be acknowledged, and expressed for humans, male or female, to become loving, fully actualized beings.

On the way to becoming a Jewish nun, a call to the Russian Steppes of the Black Sea came, to delve into the depths of my grandmothers. I entered a ferociously strong, embodied matriarchal line, that is the living will and legacy of my grandmothers. How did they survive as Jewish women? Why were they chosen out of millions who died amongst the gas chambers, and ghettos that stripped their identity, and clothed them with shame?

They were the high priestesses, shamans that nurtured and cultivated the dying bodies and spirits that were held prisoner in the walls of the ghettos, a block from their homes. In remembrance, I walked the icy cold streets of Moscow in the dead of winter. Immersed in the songs and the culture, surrounded in a foreign land, and yet I was in the dark shadow of my ancestral belly, a place where my family was persecuted and murdered for their very being and identity. They hid and were hidden in the attics and bunkers below the earth, they ascended to the heavens, in smoke.

After spending a month in the Ukraine, by the Black Sea, I was on my way to the holy land of Israel. Before I was allowed to journey onward, I was stopped in suspicion of espionage in the airport with my all encompassing black attire and baggage, just as I was detained when traveling on the night of the New Year, in the streets of Moscow.

Cheering upon landing is the ritual done on Israeli airline El Al. It is a welcoming cheer, the welcoming home of a homeless people to their homeland. I was finally home…or was I? What did I need to do to be initiated as a Crowned Virgin? I was determined to be a servant to God, and make the transition.

The transition from the star studded "whore" to the beginning of being initiated as a crowned virgin. From being a fashion model, and fully immersed in the media arts, having my own television show, and producing a talk show, to embracing the study of the orthodox Jewish tradition and its laws. The laws of "kol isha, the voice of a woman, deemed forbidden, due to its inherent quality of eroticism. In essence, it was the systematic silencing and repression of women in tradition, society, and culture, the absence of women from spiritual leadership.

I opted for the immersion into the ancient within a modern scope, and whatever it fractured or healed in its wake. For it was time to remember, that which had been forgotten. From within the depths of silence, I began to create the safe space, the vacuum I needed for remembering my lost soul. Who was she? How was she silenced? How did the death occur? I was preparing for a rebirth I was not aware of. The search for my lost soul, my soul retrieval of this and many past lifetimes, had begun.

So, the high priestess, later to be shaman guru, went underground once again. Getting in touch with the inner sacred nature of innocence in becoming the crowned virgin, a journey of inner vision was pulsating, and its voice was very loud

Walking, waking, watching, hitchhiking, riding the bus, cab rides in fear of dying ...

I am Holly Hare, and my story evolved from a dark passageway – a hollow feeling of death, a comprehensive shaking and numbness of inner body feeling, emptying out of and into a radiant emergence of what is sacred, what is woman, what is man, what is ecstasy.

Each side has a story……each side has lost much…for me

running past a bomb outside my home… I was saved from a

bomb in a cell phone

On the street

….to kill…

A dear friend 7 months pregnant waiting at a bus top in the

West bank-

In Gush Etzion – stabbed

With a knife to her back

As she falls – the blade just missing the area where she and

her baby would have passed...

These are the miracles and some of the stories that lie in the

hearts of ours—all of ours.

Before he left one of the Palestinian journalist men, asked me

not to forget one thing...

That they do want peace ...

Calling for peace, I asked myself what is meant by a call for peace, by whom, a land of peace, and what actions must be taken, to be authentic, and in my own heart, while taking stand for who I am and what is true?

Inside the vision of war,

I surrender to visions of peace

Peace inside of mind

Peace inside of body

Peace inside of soul

I surrender to the power within

As the power

Of peace

I turn to the vision of gratitude as a means of peace

I turn to the vision of community as a means of peace

I turn to the vision of oneness as a means of peace

Peace is the war inside of our selves ending

Ending with a new beginning

Lab of Evil & Light

She lies on the table awaiting the news. Was she to be placed in a hole? A morgue? A continuous laboratory of evil and light?

"I lie awake at night dreaming of the time when all when be revealed. When I will know who he is and why he has come to me. Each one. Each time.

I wonder about all the eyes that have looked, That have wanted to. That wanted what they wanted, and that was all."

What exactly was it that brought the begging, praying for mercy, to be saved from this awful moment?

"Is anybody out there? Anyone there to help me?"

I asked him to be my savior, subconsciously of course, he heard my plea, and wanted nothing to do with that role. He wanted to play the role that went with the goodness, not the blues of hard earned wisdom. He was the one who showed me how to love.

Then he left. Why did any of them have to leave?

Daddy, please, daddy are you there?

Why did you have to go?

Now I do not want you to stay.

He bought the graves sites in the holy city of Tsfat, where all the or saints are buried, he thought that would be a good segula, or omen, for a wedding gift. We toured the cemetery, where he pointed out our burial mounds, on our honeymoon.

It was the fantasy I lived in tumbling down around me, one brick at a time.

What would happen to me if I stayed?

What would happen if I didn't?

I did not dare to think of the many years of looking behind my back.

No idea what I had involved myself in.

We got engaged in four days ... my third

engagement.

We had a party, he was wealthy, handsome,

intelligent, charming,

What could go wrong?

Red flags were everywhere

I was blind and could not see, did not want to see

The path I was to walk down...with my hair

covered down the streets

Of Jerusalem.

My wedding was one big masquerade…a lie a

betrayal of all I knew

To be true deep inside…yet I had no permission

to speak it.

My mentor said he was the best I would ever get,

validating her own life, her own her abuse, and so

I walked down that isle with a veil over my eyes,

and married a man that would sink poison into all

my pores.

Blindfolded and silent my dreams crashed and

shattered all around me as he broke the glass

with his foot.

Once I was in, I could not get out-without HIS

permission of course

I waited and waited like rapunzel, in an ancient house of ruin.

The ruin of my life as I knew it, my community had disappeared.

I was going against what everyone saw to be "right"

Yet I was a warrior for all women trapped

Silent, in the face of outrage and disgrace

Fighting for the freedom

Of our collective soul

I made my way into the courtroom...

The judge calls us forward

By a miracle I was released, he was about to hand me

The get

The document

I could hardly wait

The judge says: you are now free to be with any other man.

The proceeding was over

All I knew was that my soul was crying to sing

It was free

I ran into the hall, amongst all the ultra-orthodox

men and women

Rabbis and judges

I yelped at the top of my lungs, as I tore my hat

off...

That was the beginning of a long journey back to

my true self.

Sleeping with the Devil

Where sadness and anger are seen

and heard

As Holy Awakening

Created before the dawn of time

It is the first and only game

Where the player, hero, obstacles

Enemy, goal, and creator are One.

It is changing every second

and has clues everywhere to reach

the next level filled with terrifying lows

and unimaginable highs.

It can only be won.

There are no ties

or losses

and it is about to end at any moment.

His eyes were coming from the wrong place. He was the

scorpion pretending to be harmless. The dark scared of the

light. The light no longer scared of the darkness within.

Dancing through the darkness to get through to the light;

The light;

the war, the bars

Melting

No longer a prison

A place where the unknown is revered, not feared.

A place where the mundane is sacred,

the sacred revered.

War is forgetting that we are Human.

To forget you are only human, to think you can act like a God, this is the opposite of reverence. An irreverent soul is one who is not able to feel respect for people, they see others as lower than themselves.

We met at the juice bar. Detoxing, cleansing, rejuvenating. Drawn like a moth to a flame, he wanted what as in my eyes.

The light. Yet, that very brightness is what scared him. He knew I was not pretending to be good.

He called himself a pot millionaire. Someone who would always be a champion for crime. I mean, whoops, pot crime that is. Although it was legal in California, he was in Texas, on a mission to collect. How did the money loop him into my soul contract?

We danced skin against skin, until he told me he was the devil.

In my bed, this man admitted to this lovely piece of

information. He had shown me his darkness. I was done, with

the contract.

Done with the power men held over my life. Done with the

darkness that was staring me in the face.I was done sleeping

with the devil. Power without reverence is a catastrophe;

Aflame with arrogance.

Service without reverence is smoldering towards rebellion.

From internal rebellion, we dream our visions and look to the

future

To you born into violence

The wars of the red ant are nothing;

You, in the heart of the eruption, to you the machine guns

To you the semen of fire,

The birth of the maggot in the corpse, You, to whom we send

these gifts;

At the heart of light we are crushed together.

When the sun dies we will become one.

Inside my heart

I surrender to the vision of Unity

Where souls are all we see soul love

The other becomes invisible to the mind's eye … the soul

becomes visible.

A place where loving is the vision of peace.

A vision of rebirth being born anew, as vision of life

as sacred.

You and I, are we fighting the same war?

Then why do you lie on the telephone?

Your voice fuzzy with a hint of guilt?

If the enemy is north, why do the guns point at my house?

Why do you study karate instead of artillery warfare?

Two generals command the armies of their bodies,

fainting, withdrawing, attacking. If it is the same war,

Are you sure we're fighting on the same side?

The same body, the same soul

Are we truly one?

Are we truly human?

Were we not made in the image of G-d?

Do we not have the body of the Goddess?

Are we not the memory that we hold, our body knows and

remembers?

The bite came and went, the choice to join the other side, the scorpion at my door was a warning, keep your eyes open.

Intertwined legs, links hearts, and carries minds away from the daily task

Or does it?

To love

To destroy

What appetizer shall it be tonight?

How shall we agree to play the game this afternoon?

How will our meetings go?

do we fight for pleasure or pain?

What do we vision into our lives?

War or peace, or both?

Snippets of a new world,

Resurrection, Creation

Where is the love that we crave?

How have we become a love junkie?

Manifesting in global war junkies, forgetting the sacred, allowing for the profane, the veil to be so thick we can no longer see at all

The one who stands before us as a soul, that is our own flesh and blood.

They file in-13 Palestinian journalists: ten men, 3

women.

Each one pays their respects, and bows to share and receive

you

We stand liberal Jews of Anti Defamation League; to the left

Of the round wooden table.

Flowers and food divide us, stares and glances connect us;

History, war-filled smiles and hearts await, anticipate talk of

torturous blood stained memories; Worn by so many in this

house, some in theory and some in experience.

Groups begin to form, and questions thrown. Straight,

sideways, in a diplomatic effort, to do what I am not sure.

You must trust in your heart of compassion and theirs, your understanding and theirs, you must trust your heart to speak your truth and theirs, for both of us have been struck by daggers whose wounds lie deep and bleed deeply, call each other, crying out in pain...

Why do we have to shed our skins to remain alive on the land that is ours...

Why must you perceive us as less than humans....

Why must you teach your children to hate the Jews and proclaim not one does?

Why must you say no one has intention to drive the Jews into the sea and blow children's brains out on unexpected buses I traveled on, streets I treaded...

Why must we have to be in our towns by 6 p.m.?

Why can I not travel as freely as I would like?

Why must a wall be built on my family's farm?

Why do you call Israel Palestine? Why do you ask me if I believe in the UN?

 Why do tears come to your eyes as I ask you why you call Israel Palestine, and then you close your heart to mine? I see you were open and willing to share, your heart and afterwards ask me what my experience was like in the West Bank.

How do I speak with you after you damn my efforts to know and understand you?

He pulls me aside.

Do you know how much it takes for me to be here in this room with JEWS.

As he asks me, I hear my own thoughts, as his words echo in my ear, as I tell a fellow Jew who does not want to believe that this man could have been lying to his face.

There are many kinds of lies called propaganda, such as the media director for the Center for Torture victims who states that 99 percent of all torture is done by Israelis, as the another invites me to Ramallah within earshot, where two soldiers were violently murdered, tortured and hung for all to see, on display for the Italian media who was there to Broadcast it last year.

How can we believe such men as they tell of ideology that is written in their holy text of the Koran to annihilate the Jews? The writing that I have seen with my own eyes, and with a Muslim translator, translating the walls that say exactly such desires, in the old city of Jerusalem, as I walk by them, each day going as I go to pray at the western wall.

I walk by words of hate and destruction of the Jews again, and yet I trust to come to this home after four years of living side by side in Jerusalem and in both Gush Etzion and the Shamron which is about 20 minutes from Ramallah.

I came to open my heart and have compassion as they did come, we must have compassion and understanding for all hearts hurting, and bleeding, although we must be educated as to the history of the land, and not give away our souls, which is deeply connected to the land of Israel which G-d gave to the Jewish people, thousands of years ago as well as in recent years.....

By miraculous war victories where Israel acquired the land the Palestinians were living on...as in all wars.

Land is acquired, there is no occupation, there is no colonization...

For as the United States acquired California from Mexico,

As did Israel acquire was then called Palestine.

One Palestinian journalist says to me this night,

Colonization must be ended in order for peace to happen.

Let us be clear that we must not allow our faith in Israel, the land of the Jewish people to be forgotten and treated as though it were for sale. We are not for sale, we deserve a homeland as do other nations. We must remember what occurred just fifty years prior when we, the Jewish people did not have a homeland and were dispersed all over the Diaspora when all countries denied access to those survivors, waiting in harbors to be admitted, after waiting to die in concentration camps, in humiliation again.

We say never again, but how can we lose faith in our people and in our land just 50 years after so many tried to cleanse us from the planet. The Arabic nations have many lands they may go to. We must not sell our soul that was murdered 6 million times, our collective soul, that is bound and tied to the land of Israel for and forever more. In doing so we must remember that our Palestinian neighbors have hearts, and families and pain and anguish as we do. We must have honest conversations and not make nice, when we are destroying hundreds of thousand of lives with the sale of land, and not taking a stand, being pushed around by so many all over the world.

Sacred Intimate

The war of life seems to be ravaging my eyelids, inside of my skin. Looking inside of the luminescent rays that color my internal organs. He asks me if a soul could be cleansed, and I am wondering how far away from needing a soul cleanse was I. How close was I, am I, to joining the other side? The dark side? How close am I to becoming a sacred intimate?

Becoming the table upon which men eat their sushi. The table that has no name, or a name that is not mentioned, except for cherry. Can one look inside of a cherry table which sushi rests upon?

If I was sleeping with the devil, who was he sleeping with? The Goddess.

How thankful was he to be in my presence, until I would not give him the name. A name. Any name, the name of my ex-husband. My walls went up as he pushed further and shamed me for my boundary.

Withholding, at least he let me know he was the devil. He did not remember revealing himself as such a week later.

His Memory. Twenty years of drugs. Gone.

Did I really bring him closer to the light? Heal him in anyway?

Why did he come? To test me and my loyalty to God-light?

How the river flows with incongruity. My life seems to meander and wind along this endless road of shame and abuse. With glimmers of light here and there. As each day goes by I wonder how to maintain my faith in people, in Spirit, in all that I have dreamt and dream.

My eyes fall heavy, as the emotional weight of last nights episode of invasion is equivalent to a massive hangover.

The wheatgrass gives me a little help, a small jump start.

I am lying naked on my white comforter, the dog and I asleep. She starts barking. I wake in a daze from deep dreaming and throw some covers around my bare skin. She is quickly approaching me without warning, carrying a white envelope in her right hand.

I tell her to wait until I put some clothes on, while she continues charging up the stairs. This will be your last month here she says.

I walk back into my space in a glazed panic, as the anxiety builds rapidly, I sit and stare into nothing. Nowhere that is where I feel I have landed. After years of searching and healing, remembering, and empowering my core, I on the outside looking in, I am in the same damn place as I have been for the last four years.

So what is on the inside. All that I have gained, the bankruptcy, the love? Where is it? Oh, I know it is inside of me. That's it. I remember now. Whenever I need to gain support it is always right there with me.

Yes, And how do I eat again?

Should I sell my body? Does that order come with a soul? Attached or as a side order?

An hour remaining to make a decision. Pressure. What to do next? These bits and pieces of new lives I have been starting all over the US and abroad. When will that end? When will a new life of stability and security, peace, and love begin?

The edge has become lame. I prefer the middle of the yoga mat now.

The deeper the breath the deeper I go into my peace and sweat which brings up my rage. Which brings into existence my fire? Fire. I have channeled the fire into addiction for so long. The addictions, all of them, are sweating out. I am ready to be with a man, with a man, as a woman, as a partner, as a friend. Give him to me. Now.

I thought my time of being alone was over.

Apparently not.

As the scorpion waited by my door, and the tick bit me that night, I knew that the demonic powers of the dark night of the soul was both empowering and unraveling something within me that had been left tangled and twisted in a knot lined with red golden silk. That is the complexity that shows up in cleaning out the intestinal track. Taking out the many feet of intestines and placing them on a table only to open their insides, and clean them out, so all may flow easily and smoothly. I am preparing for a cleanse today, yes, another one.

In the midst of the madness he left all the planning up to me. I was given an unlimited bank account to draw on and from. He was watching to see what I would do. He loved to watch me. Through the windows, as I dressed in the shades, he made sure to close all the curtains so no one else would be privy to his special view. His special vixen, age nine.

What an initiation to come into the world with.

He is now watching me from a distance, having his friend follow me from state to state. My ex-husband. I say I am a lesbian to release the dark energy of chains that lay around my feet. The legacy of dark exceptions to the rule of no escape, no bondage from the reality of mystical sanity. He was the devil sent to me. He invaded my life, and then I replayed the scenario to remember and not forget what happened to my soul.

She rules the dark night, the sexual night of Eros. Yet, the light of her soul, rules the day and wants to play with the innocence she has lost and deeply retained through her mother's eyes. Which were so innocent once? Once the dark seed had been planted inside of her it was not long before the seed started to be watered and grew wildly. Grew out of control, and yearned for more water.

The sweet garden.

I was driving over to San Diego to begin my doctoral studies, when I felt something on the left side of my head. I reached up to touch the feeling I had, when it jumped to my third eye. Swerve. I almost hit the side wall with my light turquoise Lexus convertible. I felt like Audrey Hepburn with the top down, and the colorful scarf tied around my head. Although in this moment, all I could do was scream, and regain my composure as the lizard jumped from my heard onto the floor. I was paralyzed, yet had to move forward. I felt as if it had just jumped down my throat and I could not utter a word.

It was stuck in the depths of my larynx. I was silent, held my breath, and prayed for the lump in my throat to be removed by some brave man at a gas station. I pulled over, and asked the first large man I saw to grasp the lizard off my floor. He cowered and said he was afraid. So, I got back on the road with this lizard in my car, and drove to my new destination.

A warning. A sign. Yes, both. All the above.

Soul Grabbing.

The snaky snake feeling of a man trying to possess you, own you, own your soul.

I sensed money coming from over yonder. Knew he was Jewish. A Jewish Richard Gere. He says he knew I was also Jewish, right away as well. What gave it away I thought? I thought he would become one of my clients, and he thought I would become one of his, and then work in his office. It turns out that we were two souls meeting to hug each other in a pure way.

He was one of those men, so rare that had the clean energy around him. A 28 year-old client who invited him to her home to show him her spending addiction, a collection of shoes and purses, though he declined.

The core of addiction is your soul trying to grab itself back into the body, collecting the pieces that had been stolen or missing.

We ended up being able to share and give each other hugs. Even though I would have liked a loan, and he would have liked to have me on his team.

Loneliness suffocates my palette, longing for the soothing of emotion through loveless sex. The lens through which I began seeing my own inner life was a pan of the dark shadows that I have been a witness and participant to. I have divulged the secrets of my soul to no one in particular and to everyone who is someone. Which is no one really? I have only begun to realize that the mystery that people see in my skin is the nakedness I wish to reveal to all who see me.

Do I wish to remember the depths of darkness which have provided me with a a unique lens to view the world, how the goddess has summoned me to speak
Her wisdom?

Although all roads seem to lead to the same standstill as

opposed to still point. Where does the lure spin into a continuum of spider webs dancing in the sunlight waiting for the moon's rise?

You know I just got out of prison don't you? There was insanity mixed with love, fear, and hate, goodness in his eyes that make the heavens shake and roar, another eviction, an episode of being fired from the post. Another feeling of we don't want you. You are no good.

So we push, and wait for the flower to dip its virgin self into the glass teacup and watch as it unfolds love at first sight, opening and blossoming in a bubble womb of warm water. Two blossoms shoot through the air, spring forth with a reddish pink flower in the center symbolizing the heart which connects two beings.

When the heart is not connected the two souls wobble as there is nothing to bind them. The entire entity floats as one world, although separate, surrounded by the green living organisms

embracing the elements of creating life.

Exile of Soul, Body, Mind

The felt disconnection we have from our bodies, our holy temple, is the exile of the soul. The exile of the soul is the exile of the feminine, the goddess.

The practice of reverence is allowing spirit goddess to channel life force through us. Dance was the sacred the pathway, the tunnel to the divine, in ancient days, every country had divine symbols representing women in their roles as spiritual leaders, healers, shamans, ritual dancers, instrument players, and singers.

In Greece, one of the oldest examples of the dancing priestess was found in an Ice Age cave painting in which the archaic goddess Boeotia stood in the center of the ring of the dancing women performing a dance of energetic regeneration rites. In Spain, an upper Paleolithic cave fresco (10,000 B.C.E) from Cogus, pictures nine women performing the celestial circle dance, or Dance of the Hours. Paintings on Sassari Sardinian, Sicilian, and Ukrainian vases and vessels from 4500 to 4000 B.C.E show figures shaped like hourglasses, wearing fringed skirts, ritual belts, and earrings. Some dance in a group circle holding hands; others dance alone or in pairs.

The ecstatic union experienced was the opening of allowing the merging and emergence of soul-union and ultimate marriage between the goddess and her groom. This was a time when the living embodiments of priestess in the temples were revered as living embodiments of the sacred feminine of the divinity in all living beings and all creation.

In temples all over the ancient world, where patriarchal conquest, took over the legacy of female leadership in ancient societies of ancient Europe and the Mediterranean. The legacy was left in the forms of tens of thousands of female figurines, hundreds of female ceramic temple models in the form of a woman, and thousands of vessels shaped as woman or painted with female figures, often dancing.

Female shamanism was most likely a collective function of the whole community in service for the sake of the whole. Women bleeding and birthing together provided a profoundly magical, vibration field in which men, women, and children, could participate in the healing and regeneration of the whole tribe.

The transition from priestess to performer, speaks of the times when the priestess was a part of the community as the grandmother. She was a nurse, midwife and healer, without being set above or elevated to priestly heights. Over time, priestesses as keepers and leaders disappeared with the rise of the priestly caste.

Space

Invisible to whom?

Out of the invisible, the visible is born. What do we want to make visible?

Dance as an integral part of woman's spiritual practice shared a parallel fate with the priestess. As religions grew further and further away from communal participation, the priestess led nature dances, dances of religious ecstasy, while fertility and birth dances were frowned upon and eventually forbidden.

A few religions incorporated the priestess as a sacred dancer into their rites, but these religions made sacred dancers servants of the temple and its priests. Sacred prostitution and the sacred marriage were known rites in the Temple of Solomon, administered by the Priestesses of Asherah, also known as Astarte, Anat, or Qedasim.

The goddess handles the snake without fear, showing she in control.

The connection of serpents with the earth and/or underworld is another important component, which may be coupled with its ability to shed its skin and characteristic of being dormant in the winter, reappearing in late spring from the earth. The snake is a terrifying creature coming from the underworld, but it has at the same time, positive connotations of renewal.

In the Egyptian religion serpents combine all of these different functions: they can be scary guardians, creators, underworld guardians, mediums of renewal, and monsters to be overcome.

The symbol for the Minoan goddess can be found mainly on the walls of the West wing in the palaces in Minoan Crete. During some time spent in the Santa Fe desert, I began drawing this symbol in a continuous fashion until it's outpouring spilled onto my walls and into my paintings, drawing large snake goddesses in a garden, as well as multicolored symbols of the Minoan goddess. My personal connection, to this symbol I was still unaware of. Still, I felt an insatiable desire to know what was desperately trying to be conveyed.

During this time, goddesses began coming into full form from my artist's brush onto the canvas with both oil and acrylic. They were Athena, Asherah, and many more. Starting to make the connection between them and a symbol on my neck that has been there since birth. It is clearly a formation in the snake shape of the Minoan symbol for the goddess. First seen as a tattoo on a classmate's leg, and having since found these to be Minoan symbols of ancient Crete.

The cult objects of Asherah, namely her golden serpent or tree symbols called asheras, are noted to have been in the Temple of Jerusalem. Asherah was said to have been the mother of over 70 gods. She was recognized by her Hathor style headdress, and stood upon the back of a lion, holding a lotus plant in her right hand, and a serpent in her left. This picture draws a direct parallel with the Minoan Faience Snake Goddess, who is shown in many temple repositories in the palace in Knossos Greece.

Seal impressions and gold rings from Mycenae and early Greek pithos found in a tomb at Knossos reveal the essential nature of the Minoan Goddess as one who is a nurturing Goddess of nature.

The Minoan Goddess has either animal servants or worshippers mainly of the female sex, worshippers of Asherah were queen mothers who wove the royal garments for Her, as well as the ones with economic and political power. A number of queen mothers are cited in the Old Testament as having served in the temple, from Bat Sheba all the way down to Mary, the mother of Jesus, and her tribe who made cakes for the Queen of Heaven.

These priestesses were not involved in sexual intercourse as ritual prostitution. They were involved in these rites to ensure the fertility of the land, as in the Eleusinian mysteries, the 9 day ritual of honoring the Greek Demeter and Persephone, and the celebration of the harvest, as in the Jewish festival of Sukkoth, all of which happen at the same time each year.

The first constructed temples were outdoor platforms built near cemeteries where dancing is believed to have taken place.

These temples, created on the hearth, were moved into temples built as separate edifices, where ritual became the domain of select individuals on behalf of the community. They once included a sacred ground, a circle of stones, a cave, or a sacred grove of trees. Organic rituals became prescribed religion. As ritual became structured and institutionalized, so did the sacred space in which worship and ritual was practiced.

Once women danced for the goddess; now they were forced to entertain the prince. The momentous split of the artistic form of worship and the devotional set a split between the sacred and the profane, caused by the social division of priests and worshippers, into masters and servants.

Devotional dances gradually became commissioned works for enjoyment of paying or ruling spectators, for provocative entertainment. Dance was transformed from a religious act or ceremonial rite into a work of art intended for observation and judgment by the observer. From these changes arose a culture of dance as theater and entertainment.

In ancient India, every major temple supported a number of priestesses who worshipped the deities through their ritual dances. These women were known as Devadasis, a word meaning female servants of God. As in many other places, these priestesses were the most highly educated women. Besides dancing, they studied reading, writing, scripture, mythology, mantras, rituals, meditation, singing, music, and healing.

Indian temple dance is one of the most beautiful fruits of the Tantric tradition. Revered as embodiments of the Goddess, the Devadasis were highly skilled in the erotic arts, and men vied to make love to them. To make love to a Devadasis was to reenact the sacred ritual of creation.

Women held high positions, and were buried with rich artifacts in the central place of honor in the tombs. Their leadership in these rites and rituals which they developed and performed can be inferred from the evidence of objects found between their legs such as a golden goblet, found in a tomb of the Scythian's, as well as potable altars and mirrors, associated with the office of the female priestess in later times. Burials of high ranking women from the Bronze and Iron ages have been found all over the Russian steppes and have been identified by archaeologists as priestesses. The shaman high priestess and her accoutrements were found from the Black

Sea, where my mother and grandmothers were born and lived, to the Altai and Tien Shan Mountains.

The mirrors were sacred objects to reflect the deepest longing and fulfillment found in divine connection. Mirrors were found among the sacred objects buried with priestesses around the world. They were used as the reflection of Divinity found within. Mirrors were worn on costumes as a reminder of the inherent soul dwelling inside: inside the garb, inside the body, and inside the temples that were destroyed.

They were also used as a reminder of external beauty, as written in the Old Testament, when in the fields, women used the mirrors to look at, with their husbands, which re ignited a spark and arouse desire in the face of enslavement while in Egypt. tYahweh and Asherah were worshipped side by side in the first holy temple of Jerusalem.

As men looked into their own mirror, and realized the power they did not possess, they decided to shatter the mirror of the Goddess. With the shattering of the vessel, the womb, the container for Spirit to dwell within, the world was left in pieces and holy sparks were strewn across all lands in the world. As with the dispersion of the Jewish people, the Jewish Diaspora began with the breaking of the vessel, the first temple in Jerusalem.

With the insurgence of male inferiority, domination began to demand the destruction of the cults of Asherah and any graven images and statues of her.

Along with the destruction of the first temple of Jerusalem came the destruction of the goddess. In exile and repression, the veils were many as She went into hiding. The connection was broken; the war was raging and waged within the inner walls. The walls were broken. The wailing had begun. The cry for homecoming, the coming home to heart...

A priestess, she knows that beauty is food for the soul. She also knows the healing power of gentle touch, caring attention, and of a sympathetic listener.

Sublime definition of creation having been divined by high priestesses around the world, in a trance they vision what is the seed they know. The seed that has been rooted, planted, and then nurtured by ancestors called forth in this lifetime-- ancestors of the goddess, ancestors beyond the realms of space and time. Honoring the goddess nature within, we see our own inner light bounce and dance forth through our brilliance. We must allow our creative brilliance to shine through in many differing spirals, as wave-spells billow forth underneath silky sway skies.

Who is the priest or priestess that is you? Who is the priest or priestess sitting in front of the mirror I wear and see before me? From where does she come? How does she come forth into my mind, into the world of woman, femininity, and divine feminine goddess life form? What is the shape of your face, your body; how do you sway and dance in the moonlight's glow?

How do you call out to the mother, daughter, infant, goddess, child? How do you call your partner? How is your partner to be called? Is your partner of this realm, are you from a realm afar?

How do you know what you know? How does the knowledge come forth into wisdom, into knowing? How do you allow for it to stream down from the heavens? Does it erupt from within the earth? Do the winds blow it closer? Do you need to open your ears to hear the whispering winds...

What is the language you speak? How may I call you? How is it you like to be called? How will you hear me? Where are you to be found? Inside of me, and everything you see, I hear your call and answer your prayers. I send you the healing before the rebirth, the death inherent in all transitions.

You must trust deep within the holy temple of spirit; you must hear your own call, speak your inners, bring forth your power to divine and breathe my name.

Tantric Temple

The rivers are wildly running, and I know that I must feel free

enough in my soul to feel free enough to commit to one person.

With my whole SELF. As they say, as he says, the man from

Montana, the trout roper who has dark locks as his mane and fish as his antlers.

Screaming, piercing, screeching, laces the night sky at the tantric temple, rage burns through my veins no more, as it reminds me of the way I have been living my life. It is a death-defying cry for life itself. A cry that screams to set me free from this torture, this battlefield of pain is excruciating, get me out of HERE. Where is here? Everywhere I am. In my body, in my mind, in my heart, in my soul, I scream to be free. To be let out of the prison that has confined me. Free from the vultures and attack that has given me the fight and struggle of many lifetimes. The Kali energy is leaving me, it is the final cry, the universal piercing of our soul exiled. An ignorance, of the core energy that sustains us and lives inside of our bodies.

We essentially walk the earth as zombies in our own skin. We numb and pump our bodies with poison and wonder why we are addicted to money, and are not aware of this fact. *Addicted to buying life energy*. Addicted to the skin that is false to feed our infatuation with numbing the screaming soul, dying, literally to be seen.

We must pay heed to the souls warning. It will not give up on us and will continue calling.

The screams mixed with soothing sounds of waterfalls give the perfect example of the way we are living in our daily lives. Giving the illusion that all is well, yet deep inside we are screaming to be seen and heard for who we really are.

We mask and cover our true selves with mascara and fancy cars, when all we really want is to be loved, and feel the connection to something greater than we are. The truth of universal sacred connection. Energy connection, the love that pervades and surrounds us always. Yet, all we see and feel is the lonely faces in the mirror and on the streets. We are a country that is desperately trying to reclaim that which is already inside of our own bodies. The breath that is sacred, that is life, that is healing, is free.

The wake up call is now. It is the most important call you will

ever receive in your life. Make sure you answer it.

It was one of those rare moments, I will never forget.

It is a wail of horror, at what has happened or is happening, that everyone has watched as it occurred. *A sexual holocaust of the soul.*

The holocaust was a collective murdering of the soul of the shechinah, the divine feminine face of god. The feminine within all of us. The wailing still continues in the face of the full moon. It is an unbearable cry, as though a mother is watching the children she conceived and gave birth to being murdered before her eyes. Unbearable and unstoppable.

Healing. There must be a way to heal.

Loving the masculine and feminine within your core.

How does she show up? He?

Her lovemaking sounds bring my orange sun on the horizon to new awareness. What if they were sounds of the earth mothers pleasure? Harmonious deep succulent peach pleasure, which we deny ourselves each day. How can we heal pleasure?

Pleasure in our daily lives? How can we abundantly give in to our yearning and desires to ourselves, and the worlds around us?

By dancing your masculine and feminine aspects we open to our true divinity of non-duality, as both energy forms are found in one body. Our soul has both masculine and feminine sides. Our womb is the space where we hold all of our wounding, the gate to the temple.   The door to the sacred heart. Our heart of all hearts. The secret to healing pleasure.

  Join us in this walk to enter the temple gates, hand in hand... Working to unclothe the mystery streaming forth from within the inner layers of clothing hiding the gift of joy and love inside the soul of home. Within home lies the deep pleasure we seek. How can we get in touch with our deepest yearning?

The yearning that is available to all of us lies hidden in the treasure box of our bodies, and our souls. We must awaken this treasure chest so the ballerina will dance her soul dance. Her deepest passion. We must lay each piece of clothing to the side as we open the doors to true pleasure and the gift of loving. Loving our bodies as ourselves. Loving that which is present in our layers of disease, and pain, lies the quintessential essence of divinity. The love we give to ourselves and have for so long denied the joy and life of freedom to receive pure love. Touching the depth of oneness inside our soul is the way to our heart. Our heart is the one place in our bodies which connects all of our centers. It is the hub of feeling, feeling well. Our brain is the center for processing all that we feel, coming to awareness of what our heart is saying to us.

Our soul is the place where all the information, spiritual and physical DNA is stored and flows from. The memories of all past is contained in the particles, the quantum energetics of the realms traveled by all of us, even if we are unaware of them at the time or not.

The soul is the water where all is connected and activated. It is the dreaming of our new lives and new selves that will be brought forth through the erotic. Through the divine pleasure we begin to learn how to receive. When we begin living from a place of clear heart passion we will begin to see clearly how to manifest all of what we want. It will come from the first chakra of foundation and upwards to our passion, and power. It will then travel to our heart, and then our fifth chakra, where we express all of our emotion, gratitude, hatred, anger, and love. It is the blue essence of where our truth meets our integrity and action. It then travels up to our third eye where all illusion and truth is seen and must be deciphered and filtered through. Then breathing all up through to Father Sky, and back down again to Mother Earth. This energetic rainbow lineage is used to transmit and transmute all that has been emerging, changing, and growing all through our bodies and spirits.

As I walked my grandmother through her last time in nature I knew I was priestessing her death and voyage onto the next realm. As I was taking another step on mine. She was able to see the waters below and the beauties of the forest and trees. She asked to lie down on the altar above the scene which could have easily been Fiji or Hawaii, although we were in cheese country Minnesota. As she was preparing to be a holy sacrifice, I told her how she is one of the few who is leaving the world having given only good to its transformation and growth. She smiled, as we held hands, and I could feel how close to death she and I were. We were one in the moment, andI sensed the fragility and preciousness of life and how at any moment we could lose our breath, our life force. The one in which we become aware of our freedom and divinity. The preciousness of life comes with the knowing and or feeling of imminent death.

Boundaries.

The guarding is to defend against someone entering the gates of the temple before one is invited. This prevents people from opening their hearts fully. The key is to hold your boundaries while opening your heart. Aligning your mind with your truest knowing and deepest desire, is the golden compass to purity, truth, and freedom.

This allows you to become the container, to become the crystal, you are the crystal. You are the healthy and clear vessel.

You are like the rising sun
Inspiring the depths through silence and desire

So this trip has been about living tantra. The living waters of learning has bestowed their grace upon me in the form of the white tigress. She is the one who speaks her truth and allows the jade dragon into her temple when and only when she desires it to be so and is ready. She is one who moves through the dance of sensuality, slowly, smoothly, and as the goddess tells her how to move.

The man who wishes to pleasure her, kiss and rub her feet is worshipping her temple, although in her heart she knows that she is not desiring him at that level. She is the sweet water, she knows she tastes different and he is salty. Not the bear lover, the one who loves to cuddle, yet her love for him is agape brotherly love, and not of sexual nature. She thinks about her desire to be touched and caressed with deep love and affection, and even though there is no emotional connection, he is willing, she thinks and so why not.

The neediness of his emotional body, the desire to worship or please, the feeling of being worthy of making her orgasm, etc, and she agrees as the massage slowly moves into a sexual tone, a sensual loving act of worshipping her yoni, and her being-ness. While in her heart she does not reciprocate and this is a personal betrayal for her. She allows herself to allow him into her emotional body when the calling is not there, it is her body calling or accepting, allowing herself to be worshipped while she leaves the other parts of herself outside the windows of choice. The inner layers of choice are the doorways to bring in the layers of truth of all the energy centers of your mental, physical, emotional, and spiritual bodies into alignment and agreement with each other.

She was left feeling out of balance and out of touch with her inner most soul, her innermost truth was hanging like the laundry on the line outside the house. Clipped but floating in the wind.

Tantra is the being-ness, being with the desire not flowing in the direction of sexual intimacy that is presenting itself, while maybe you wish the desire was matching the level of the person sitting across from you. The lesson here is about listening to the soul whispering a full yes or a full no at every turn. The agreements your energy centers are communicating, whether positive or negative, are constantly sending you messages along your journey into the intimacies that spiral open and closed.

Lying in a love roll, gazing into one another's eyes, touching each other with ease and grace, allowing one to see who you truly are, allowing the acceptance and honoring of what truly is, two souls connection, communing and communicating oneness and love.

How do I want to be touched, when do I want to be touched or entered? You may not know the answer to these questions right away, although your body and soul do know. The knowledge is energetic. The knowing comes from the deepest wisdom of each living cell, that is breathing and communicating knowledge and wisdom, that is uniquely and solely your own to share and express.

This wisdom, our higher self, comes to witness our desires and our yearnings to speak our deepest desires and truths. This is the divine masculine energy which come to hold space for the creative flowing juices of the divine feminine. The divine feminine aspect is being empowered by her own sacred truth and it's expression. The truth is riding the wings of freedom. Once we listen to the heart, we activate the fifth chakra to express our wisdom. The wisdom of tantra is the weaving of energy centers to speak truth in order to live in purity and freedom, which essentially is love.

Wandering. The comfort of home. Is it to be found in a home where all is waiting for your arrival. Our soul is waiting for us to come home to it's gates.

It is our souls intention to retain the bodies restorative power and energetic wisdom to attain a union of spiritual vitality that carries us through ultimate health and wellness.

Restorative sex. This is the power to cultivate your life giving energies to enhance youth and vitality. Through the arousal of erotic energy you cultivate the movement of the body's innate wisdom and power to restore itself, heal itself. By moving the body to arousal a woman brings the yang or masculine energy she needs to acquire ageless youth and vitality.

The living waters of semen and vaginal secretions are the antidote to the pleasure and pain principle that is not being met in our culture. We answer to the call of our bodies by numbing the reactions of the soul body crying out to be heard.

We bow in deference and in reverence to our mothers and sisters to crown our selves self-sovereign. We are the ones who say how and when our bodies are called to serve in a way we are called to serve.

Inside the wisdom of a woman's body lies the innocence and intensity of her sacred womb. Her sacredness has been the reward of the generations of eternity... She will enjoy her energy body merging with her lover and partner through conscious loving, intuitive, blissful union as she is beheld as the sacred vessel and living bastion of compassionate light and devotion. She is the embodiment of all elements divine that bring into reality the ideas, and desires of the male divinity;

A woman's energy is gathered.

It nearly drove me insane, being called insane all the time,

crazy and spiritual. Fauna. I drove to town with my headlights

off, and somehow they always seemed to be turned on. On,

Turned on, am I. Always. Just sitting there in the café, my body

feels like gyrating and making love to someone NOW. What

can I do, no one in sight to touch?

At the end of my rope, I have chosen the path of the few. How

did I get here? By following my heart? By following the road to

the promised land, the dream, my dream? I didn't settle for any

of the twenty proposals for marriage I received? Why am I

struggling now?

Done with selling ice cream, done with the scooping, and tired

of asking my mother for money. Why should she have to

sacrifice any more?

Guilty. Intensely Guilty. She send more. To control, to convict, to absolve herself.

Deciding whether to use a glove while she massaged men.

Erotic touch was something she had never thought about, not yet anyway. Now she had taken the plunge, and was deciphering how to hold her boundaries in tact.

My friend Sophie, went through many levels and layers of unfolding her own being through this process that would take her deeper into herself.

Would she be able to sustain her soul purity? He says no. The pot millionaire, who wants to cleanse his soul. He says she will not be able to do this.

What do these two people have in common? He wants to cleanse his soul of all the sins against humanity he has committed and she wants to be the vehicle. Is she able to cleanse him? Can he cleanse himself through her? Were they meant to meet to fulfill a prophecy?

The hidden secret that was her own. That was still hidden from her own mind. She thought to herself, her, oh no. Not her.

Taking people on journey into the unknown sensual and sacred was not what she went to school for. It is what she became? Was it her destiny?

War: Our true story

As war encircles our planet, we rise to greet the moon.

The moon dances around the sun, merging emergence of soul love.

Visions of Peace.

Visions of War came to me the night before the first attack in 1999.

I had just left a full scholarship at an Ivy league University, being called to the holy land many times before, and this time asked to stay, and journey through the cycles of the sun and moon.

It was Rosh Hashanah, the Jewish New Year, and I was spending it with the Rabbi who I would come to know as family, teacher, mentor, and friend. In a sense already had. He and his family lived in the Shamron, or West Bank. I was in a bullet proof bus on my way there, having visions of what was to haunt my daily life and future dreams.

The bits and pieces started to come back in waves, in esoteric blips on a panning screen, I was there, I was living in fear. Those healing dreams were mine to remember. I had lived through a war. I have lived through a war. The reality is setting in. Los Angeles seems like Disneyland. My world is being flipped upside down once again. Where am I? Where have I been? Where have I landed?

He was drawn to me. He made me laugh. His light was contagious. He held me in times of crisis. He was a religious Muslim.

One night we sat down and he asked me about the soul, the feminine soul...we had a beautiful discussion which led into our origins...ours his, and my story. He asked me to accompany him on several occasions, to many different locations and events, I smiled, and sweetly declined. Although I had a sense we were to create something together.

I was driving down to Los Angeles, for a conference.... A vision of a moon dancing around a sun came to me, singing songs of peace and prayers of love. When open mic time came at the university...I asked if he wanted to play some music with me...he agreed and we improvised deep prayerful energies into the night...on the stage, out into the community and world…we were in and creating a vision of peace on that stage.

Most importantly we were souls sharing loving-kindness.

The plans were being made….they were to have a healing circle for one side, one sister, one view, which was the beginning of my alienation, and another transformative heart opening.

A healing circle at another university I attended. As the night fell into sky, my heart began to turn inside out as I questioned whether to attend the healing circle for a Lebanese sister. As I sat in the healing circle feeling my pain, as hers. At the end of the circle, I got down on my knees, and sang to her heart, my heart, for our healing, for our pain, for our experience, for our fears, in love. Spontaneous ritual, releases the ego, allows the love to flow in from spirit to spirit. Sister to holy sister, in humanity, we sit in a circle, that cannot be filled with silence it must be filled with reverence for another human being, another soul life, living, please goddess in their heart.

I have been applying and applying since I have been back from the holy land, Israel. Interviews…shaming…no calls…I'm done with it. The take over by the coup…the rotten remains I was left to bear, picking up the corpses and blood left by believe it or not the holy ultra orthodox sect in Los Angeles.

She calls me in to shame me for my inconsistency of my gypsy-ness over the years, and says she will need to do a background check and references if she is to hire me. Little does she know that I would not work for her sorry belittling behind even if she was paying in golden apples.

Does the crying mess, me, go on? NO, I am not carrying on like a hurt baby, I am a sensitive woman, that has had a tough, very tough ride. Even though some point out how "easy" I have had it. Easy? Did not think that one described my life at all.

Life. What is it all about? Learning to love your neighbor as yourself.

We could all just stay children, better yet babies.

I guess it is all about remembering what we already knew when we knew. Back then. When our eyes glistened of divine knowing as we came out of the birthing canal, those oh so holy waters.

Back to the womb space, back to the breath, where is that knowing now?

He writes that his life is not his own. What about mine? Is your

life your own, if you cannot pay your bills? Put food into your

mouth without putting out?

So here I am. Living the life of a starving artist slash housewife

without the house and without being a wife. Maybe a mother to

my five pound Chihuahua. Thinking about turning my life into a

play. The script has already been written…or has it?

Where do I search for answers? When all is a mystery and a

secret waiting to reveal itself. There is always a way. Always.

What I deserve? The dream last night reminding me, someone did love me once. That purity was there, is there, if I call it forth in the present.

I deserve to sleep with a God, a Priest, a Light being, full of love. Full of kindness, that is grateful to Spirit as opposed to the devil.

Looking at my homelessness as another opportunity to be home. To live in a way that asks for forgiveness. Innately I deserve a commitment from a man who loves my inner beauty.

Sedona feels like she is calling me, to tell me something. I must go.

Some people come into our lives quickly go. Some people move our souls to dance; they awaken us to a new understanding with the passing whisper of their wisdom. Some people make the sky more beautiful to gaze upon. They stay in our lives for a while, leave footprints on our hearts, and we are never, ever the same.

If you dream it, you can do it.

Inner core Energy

Emitting fumes, evoking ease, complacency, to build a family

How do we know, Who is the one, We will know

He will know

She will know

When they will know

At the same moment

They will chose each other's breath

To wake to love in the morning

They will know the difference between love and lust

They the former

Enjoy the latter

Emitting, emptying, dumping drama

At once

In doses

The one who is there, but not really there at all.

He wishes to be with you, with himself, although he does

Not have himself

So he chooses you to mirror him.

To create the attachment he is not ready for.

Thank you and no thank you for trying and lying

To yourself and my heart.

Energetically drawn to the one that mirrors inadequacy

Sabotaging empowerment and efforts

Reinforces what inner voice has whispered for so long

The recorded voice of the past, rewinds and relays

Finding the producer to re-record the voices

That tell me who I am

What my worth is

Without another

My higher self-love

Inner teacher loving soul self

Tells me I am love.

In love with life and Spirit.

Am I? Is all this unrealistic bullshit, new-age jargon I try to talk

myself into believing or out of?

Were they all just devils incarnate in disguise? Were they all sent as lessons? Were they the actual puppets?

Am I really free now?

What about this thousandth dark night of the soul…swimming in these waters of recycling, rebirthing, what will I give birth to next?

I feel I am giving birth and voice to some experience I have been reliving over and over. This time someone is listening.

Turning off the radio and pushing play on the cassette recorder, although there is no script there, it is coming from my heart, no more pretending.

No more fear to be who I am.

Sexy, powerful woman, hear me roar, it's okay, I run with the wolves at night.

I'm back to wondering how close I am to being darkness if the devil decided to reveal his face to me, in my own bed, well, scared the living daylights out of me, and made me fear nothing, less.

I now see more people this way somehow. Less trusting. More trusting of the world around me…that somehow it will turn out okay…a night-sea journey…Jonah in the belly of the whale being spit out when he was ready to accept his mission…my mission…what in the world is the mission maybe I am avoiding and that is why I keep getting spit out everywhere?

Well, what else could it possibly be?
I'm thinking about doing the nun thing again, this time maybe I will be a Hindu one…try an ashram instead of a midrasha.

Although the one catch is, as I already have found, they do not cater to little doggies, and well as you know I have one, and she, is not just a little pooper scooper, she is the princess, yes she is Jewish too.

Even though I rescued her. I now realize that I have just rescued myself.

Waiting for this holy savior to do his job, was the devil in disguise I was waiting for, and he offered it all to me, differing versions of male devils, on a silver platter repeatedly, as I made myself so desperate that I would take his plea bargain, join the other side, be abused and degraded, for being taken care of. For the life you have been asking for, for a life of imprisonment, you have mistakenly labeled as freedom.

I always said neigh.

Speak to the truth, speak it as it comes, or else it will become falsity.

The light becomes dark when feared and not given space to be fully expressed.

So we're back to radical honesty. Yes, back to the basics.

Honesty. Radical huh?

Self in the Face of Change

Memories... pieces ...given away...sold as SELF....LOVE

To whom was it sold? Did we voluntarily let it go? Was it stripped from us, stolen? Were we robbed of our most precious possession? Did we ever own it? Is it still ours, if ever? Can we retrieve it? Can we begin to understand where it lies? What it is?

In the depths of our soul lies the treasure chest waiting to be opened.

Love: inner essence of our being.

How can we touch it, come close to it, communicate with it and then express ourselves form the center core? A still small voice inside, can you hear it? It's calling your name.

ERASED. BLANK. EMPTY. Where do we begin to fill our empty cups, define the borders, outline our canvas? Who and what define our personal space, does it change, if so when, and how? External outer factors have robbed us of our awareness and connection to our inner voice, our central core, our Self.

How can we define our journey to self? Where is the map of our soul? Where will it take us? To places we have never touched before or could have ever imagined existed, inside of us. The treasure chest waits at the end of the map to be reclaimed. Lost souls wait to be paired with their other half, their bodies, mind, and heart, sold in exchange for false security. They were separated in mass conflict and confusion, worlds colliding, breaking, to come back together.

Places lined with bars, upon hearts burning to get to the other side. Pieces of souls churning shattered into a million pieces across worlds searching.

Souls searching for lost bodies, in this world, in the present.

Just as in creation, the breaking of the vessels, the shattered, refractory lights beam, the expansion and contraction, the wellspring of purity, and the depths of holiness and unlimited rejuvenating energy, of untapped potential waiting to be revealed.

The unification of body and soul is a journey of deep inner work. The path I have walked on is one of inner turmoil and struggle with past, and present reality, streamlining towards the ultimate goal of liberation from suffering.

The rewards are vast, and shine like the bare sun melting all the bars, unlocking all the gates and opening all the doors that have been closed. Yearning to come closer to your true inner self, your Buddha nature, striving for truth, healing, for becoming whole, and awake, will serve as the prime foundation to drive you along the way.

A sense of deep inner commitment to locating and owning your truth, hearing and expressing your inner voice and connecting with Spirit, is the universal energy, the underlying force that allows us to persevere through surrounding mine fields, triggered at every turn.

You will need a guide that will be able to provide you with the necessary tools for the journey and will help guide you along the way. Providing a safe and supportive space where you chose your next step with direction and focus heading towards your ultimate goal-the treasure chest inside. Who decides what self is, and to whom does it belong? Is self the external body, does it belong to society and anyone who would like to buy it from us? Is it an inner part of us, that is untouchable?

What does your 'self' mean to you? Who defines it?

Brave: One who takes the journey, wherever it may take them, through the valleys of the shadows of death, the person who glows in the dark, to find the bliss of knowing Self, Spirit, and Divine Bliss in the ordinary everyday moments. It is the medicine women and men, the high priestess, the shaman, in the modern world that walks this path, paves this Way.

Without the circumstance of your life, how would you know who you are? In dying, losing your circumstance, who would you become? Of the infinite possibilities of who you have been, and who you are what would you need to know to let go of your circumstance, to let go of your life?

Lady of Ecstasy

There are innumerable myths from Europe, Middle east, Asia, Africa, and the Americas which associate serpents with everything most sacred and essential to human life: the cycle of birth and death, the mystery of sex, the interwoven trinity of health, wholeness, and holiness. The serpent is worshipped in many parts of the world as an emblem of divinity. A well-known example is the Snake dance, which the Hopi of the Southwestern United States use to invoke the rain. Throughout Africa, snakes are venerated, and in Southern India many shrines are dedicated to the nagas, the serpent-deities.

Any encounter with the serpentine energies is a step into unknown territory, outside the ego's realm of jurisdiction, a journey crossing the borderlands between our everyday reality and the great beyond. In many societies, this was a crossing guided by a shaman who knew the way. Sacred dance and movement are among the most ancient and powerful shamanic practices of crossing over, of leaving behind the realm of the everyday and entering the domain of the serpent.

Cultivating a priestess of this time, who shares a deep commitment to the welfare of one's community. A priestess's work is to guard the soul, so that its ears stay open to the song of spirit, its heart to the love of spirit, its eyes to the beauty of spirit, they are the guardians and caretakers of the community's spiritual life. Sexually ecstatic states are celebrated literally as well as symbolically in tantric and kundalini yoga, both evolving out of shamanic practices. The Sanskrit word tantra comes from the root tan meaning to stretch or to weave. Tantra is the art of weaving together the spiritual and material worlds. It is a way of realizing the divine essence through bodily experience, especially the creative force of sexuality. The Sanskrit term kundalini, meaning serpent power, and designates divine sexual energy. It describes being in control of our sexual, erotic power, independent, and free.

She begins the stirring of the soul to passion, igniting the fire within, joy, the love, the pain, the fear, and the emotion that feeds and speaks through us. The emotions are the soul's voice, the body is emotion's voice, and the dance is the symbiosis of the universal temple of the great mother goddess.

The dances carry messages of emotion. As our emotions are the messengers our soul that come through our bodies, they serve as maps to guide us through the balance and journey of the mysteries. This form of transmission is passed through from generation to generation by embodying the sacred intentions of the dance that were created many thousands of years ago, in reverence to the mother of compassion and the Great Mystery.

The dance of thirsting for you, oh great mother of compassion, as you are the fruit of what is yearned for, and the water to quench the dryness from which these syllables were created. We dance the same notes, and weave the melody; we stand in open circle and acknowledge the cyclical cycles of life, death, and rebirth; the light and dark; the sun and moon; summer and winter.

For we are your priests and priestesses: those who do your work in the world, your highest embodiment. We serve as leaders in ritual and sacred devotion, guiding community to their highest potential in ritual, healing, and transformation.

What is the role of a priest or priestess and who may become one? How are they chosen? What are their duties? The priestess of the holy dances leads the rituals and ceremonies that hold the space for the cycles of life.

In essence, the dance of life is the healing, transformative ritual that allows for self-expression, connection, healing, joy peace, unity, community, and transformation.

We ask you lead and guide us through this journey, following the flow of the river, allowing it, you, to move in and through us. To softly touch our your gentle skin, brazing and kissing with our feet, you mother earth, we caress you, and we honor and acknowledge your presence. We are eternally grateful for this dance and the breath within us.

You within us: The fire that is in our bellies and feet, the soul voice that yearns to pour forth. We know and feel our connection to you and to each other.

We move through the invocation and initiation of life passage through birthing, entering womanhood, wedding, crone hood, rites of release. We honor the memory of you inside of us, within and inside of the dance, within and inside of our bodies.

The rebuilding of memory is reclaiming the amnesia; it is the rebuilding of memory structure, of safe space. It is the remembering and reclaiming of our divinity as women, as men; remembering and reclaiming our truth, beauty, bodies, inner knowing, our history, our reverence, our respect, and our power.

It is reclaiming the adornment of our bodies. In clothing, jewelry, headdress, and stories we tell.

Feeling held in a circle of women, in attending a goddess dance retreat, this night, our faces and colors were a fusion of love and being. This night, our hearts were woven together in a unified song that spoke in the form of dance as prayer. At the end of the night, one woman came up to me as and commented that I was a rainbow, dressed as a chakra flow, coloring energy channels in the tree of life, sacred dance of life.

Wearing red suede shoes, orange pants, a traditional Mexican dress, a teal shawl I had made, and a purple scarf. Voila! The embodied chakra in my dress; my soul had chosen subconsciously my inner and outer alignment. The flow of the river was inherently inside, speaking in whispers all along my journey and had now adorned my body in joy for my heart as well as in bringing joy to others.

Our intuitive knowing and great desire for its expression comes strongly and deeply, and yearns freedom and space. Esoteric Kabbalistic mystics say that that a person will fall sick if their soul is not being allowed to express itself.

Sacred Expression

Great Mother of Compassion, we dance in your praise, we are you, we become one with you. In the dance, we dance the oneness, inside of the web, as we hold each other sacred, in reflection of what and who we are, and where we have come. The joy, the pain, the trauma that has been repressed into fading memory, comes alive with the fire in our breath, and belly, with the soul laughter from deep knowing, of you, of us.

We must let go of the old world views that came as you were crushed in the slaughter of a power struggle. Bringing you, O great mother goddess, back into awareness. Celebrating your homecoming, welcoming you into your sacred temple, our bodies, life-givers of holy wisdom.

The language we speak is yours, one of kindness and compassion, of nourishment and sustainability, of wisdom and peace. The language and wisdom that holds the space for, you, to be present and enter, coming home from exile. As we welcome you from exile we welcome ourselves back into fullness of being all of who we truly are.

Holding reverence and respect that was once held for you as you stood side by side in the holy temple, in the embrace of creation.

The acceptance of ourselves, and each other, building the loving community that was ever present before the times of war and destruction, when all lived in peace and harmony, and saw each other as brothers and sisters.

The wisdom of the sacred ritual dance holds all of us, in reverence for all, allowing us to create a sacred space to be in gratitude and connection with self, you, Great Mother of compassion, and each other.

As the spiral opened and closed, I saw and felt the womb, and knew we were giving birth to so much. Words were dancing in-between the spaces that were the lines of circle. In silence, listening to my song, and my story, the story of all of us, the collective story weaving its way around, over, in, and through.

In bridging of the gap of the sensual and communication of the soul of the highest order, the dance leader waves her small, thin piece of silk cloth to signal the movement from inner meditation, preparation, and silence to the beginning of the emergence of the new healing and transformative symbols and patterns such as the spiral, the zigzag, the circle, the crescent, the tree of life unifying with voice and sacred song, and all of us to each other as one vibration.

Root Mother

Who is our root mother? Have we asked ourselves that question? The one that fits inside of the hand that holds the answers? Who is the giver, the Creatrix of our own lives, the giver of life, our breath, our bodies, our innate inner wisdoms? Where and who is She?

Weaving the web, the tapestry of the female Buddha, who achieved enlightenment, and fiercely declared she would always be reborn a woman, her fierce commitment to rescuing others form suffering, this is her legacy, shards hold the legacy of ancient light burning into our skin, branded, holy omissions, numbers, burning into flesh, up in smoke: the legacy of a people to be vanished, the living legacy of the female Buddha, Tara, Goddess of Compassion today.

We as women hold the vessel that has been shattered, that could not be held, as She went into hiding, as the Jewish people went into the basements of their bunkers.

Called at a young age to journey into the belly of the whale

of my inner serpent, she has emerged, been quelled, looked at,

allowed to surface, and shut down for her energetic fierceness.

The maiden that became warrior, Persephone, was taken into

the underworld. Persephone, who chose to descend and take

on the responsibility that she was given, which may be seen as

fate, the destiny of transforming dark into light. She was the

maiden who became warrior, the transformer, or holy whore,

given up for service. Is this justice with compassion? Is this

initiation a sign of the serpent who is testing and challenging us

to look deeper and climb into a pit in the ground we dug for

ourselves, and stay there as a means of facing our own death?

This is a part of the braided hair: indigenous, initiation into

womanhood, into warrior wisdom. Being a woman who is a

warrior is one who takes the risks to pay heed to the serpent

and her calling, to acknowledge the serpent and face the

questions.

The ancient mysteries are our own mysteries to unveil, our

own inner secrets to uncover. To reclaim our own inner

knowing and the many ways of knowing we have repressed as possibilities. The rapid pace of our society streamlines the status quo of the rape of history. It is the omission of woman's leadership roles as high priestesses, communal ritual, religious leaders, and the oldest religion we know which centers on a woman.

How can we not question the omission of woman's history, an omission of a deity that mirrors our own image? We must take responsibility to honor our ancient hearts to remember what they have heard and know deep within their loins. What are our grandmothers asking us to do right now? How are they asking us to remember them? By doing so, what are we giving to the world and our children?

We are giving answers to the deeply uprooted souls that are trying to desperately seek a safe haven, a home, a vessel, in the war of displacement. In a war against women, a war against life. The war in Iraq was a war against the color ochre red and the pubic V, symbolizing the essence of life flow, of creation. When society is focused on a tirade of violence as a means to peace, war is waged within and without. The rape of women, the fear embedded of power and control that men have imposed inside the psyche of woman has allowed women to identify with their abusers and allow for a systematic disassociation of root memory. It is the root memory where all the answers lie, where all the submerged knowledge lies buried.

It is also where the notion of oneness is paralleled with personal creativity and its destruction. Are we solely creating to produce an outcome that another desires of us, producing the destruction of our souls, as we submerge our true heart's desire? What does our soul ask us to do? Create in the world? What is the intention of our creation? Whom do we serve in our madness of the hustle and bustle of daily life? Where do we draw the line of the rape of our souls? Where is the barrier we hold up to guard?

How do we hold each other's boundaries in a world where justice with compassion lurks in the shadows, which comes into light while learning and facing our darkness? The dark mother who nurtures our wounds asks us to return to her, by returning to ourselves, in this era of inner awakening. She asks us to remember our roots, our inner core of strength and compassion, feeling our own heart as empty, awaiting its fullness, the spilling over from abundance into another's cup. It is the filling of another's wine glass with the ancient heart of the future.

This is our mother's root calling us to remember their names and reclaim their stories as true. To embrace our own inner wisdom, as the children who wore ribbons in our hair, and badges sewn inside our sleeve, we knew who we were then. Allow yourself to embrace your inner child who is showing the way of playful abandon on this journey. Allow her Spirit to lead you into the meadows of fervor, of passionate knowing and devotion to the truth within your heart.

On the outskirts of time, you will come to know her lines and boundaries, and the stories that make up her landscape, the soul that lives in your body. Make a home for her. Make her a priority to live in this world in a compassionate ritual of healing love, welcoming her back into the garden--the garden she is waiting to re-enter. To bring in the New Year with her destiny fulfilled in union and unison with her heart's desire, with her heart in tow. With her heart in hand, ready to give and share her innermost depths, baring her soul to the light that seeks her, that has given birth to bear tender love.

Take her by the hand, and show her you know the way. Show your inner child, you will protect her now, and ask her to stay with you, by your side, and never leave you again. Ask her to honor the pain and heartache, and scar tissues that remain; ask her to forgive, and move on with an open, empty, yet full, heart of love. Be ready to live in the present as there is no tomorrow until tomorrow arrives in the present, now. Ask her to remain in the memory of alive, orgasmic awakening.

Recovering the Soul's Orgasm

Searching on a journey down a road, where a house stood waiting for me to enter, in a visionary trance during a ritual for the Eleusinian Mysteries, I was asked to go underground. I went to the basement of the house, which I now understand as the underworld, as I did while searching for Persephone. Persephone is the embodiment of the deep interior of the soul.

We experience sex as a rapturous and ecstatic seizure of consciousness. In her world, we are seized by underworld mysticism, full of physical and emotional sensation, an enriching but overwhelming loss of self and recovery of soul.

In surrendering control, we allow our ego to dissolve into the vast ocean of oneness merging into another world where your soul is able to breathe freedom into the lungs of ecstasy. The lover, who allows the waves to take them inside of the tides, drawing life with the palms of delicacy, allows for life to become lover.

The transformation Persephone underwent, the deep transition and cycle of change, life, death, and rebirth is the experience of women and men that have survived incest or childhood sexual abuse, who go on to heal themselves, take responsibility for their destiny, and become shamanic healers, transitioning souls for others as was done to theirs. The woman incest or childhood sexual abuse survivor is placed through a soul initiation of loss and recovery of memory, feeling, faith, knowledge and sight.

From childhood, innocence is taken, the healing and repair that was necessary, the abandonment of self, to survive, only to return again in forgiveness to the mother, Demeter, who did not protect her or did not know, and uncle Hades, who took her for his own, forced in reality, chosen by destiny, to become husband and lover. Persephone transmutes the role of the victim into a powerful goddess transformer. She becomes the shaman medicine woman who is the one who has experienced many deaths and rebirths.

As queen of the dead and the underworld, Persephone allows us to consider the deepest and darkest feelings and thoughts that come to mind around sex. She deepens the awareness and emotions of those she haunts.

Her downward path is a form of mysticism, for the spiritual life can be profound as well as transcendent. Sex in particular is an effective way to find the mystical depths as well as the mystical heights.

The Cave of Spiritual Perfection

We run and seek protection from divine inspection

Opening to divine persuasion of defeat

Allowing for Spirit to walk through the gate

Of adoration, longing for destiny to pull up the

shades

Pull us into the sunlight of survival

Our birthright

Why does he call in the night so?

Why does he linger in our dreams?

On the camisole he caught us in. From where

does he enter and exit in his

Sleep? Shall he become her, tonight?

Who tells the tales of sacred story, of where we

came from?

Who weaves our web of past and present? How

far do we go back?

From what world am I? How is it that I have

Sight?

Queen of the underworld

Queen of witches

Enjoying the hunt of the hunted, the arrows pierce

into hearts

To awaken truths never told, the self and body

that know and never lie

The pen he holds never writes what I want to

hear

Lays watch over the tower I sleep in

Why does he torment me so?

Compassion harkens world wide rounds

Seekers, seers speak truths awaken worlds

within

Remembering whole body ruins of wholeness

Sacred keeper of the sparrows nest

When shall you call us next to bid your duty?

We hear a voice of desire to serve

We hear our heart run to heal the sick

We see the woman mother hold the hand of time

We have passed and given over to you

Demeter passed the role of transformer, soul transitioner, to her daughter, unknowingly. It was a transmission of the Triple Goddess, embodied in Demeter, Persephone, and Hecate. The transmission was that of Self, the divine Buddha nature within.

Transmission is a form of ritual, one that is a vital element in the healing of community, and bringing it together through ecstatic states.

I see his drum out of the corner of my eye, and his beam of light with my soul sense. His smile is a laser that opens my own to shine brightly. We speak of the healing music of peace and love; he has been traveling the world to share. His love of people and the earth is clear. We speak of going into the trenches, refining the warrior within, to then go ing into the underworld and raising the sparks of lights that were shattered and lie dormant in the night sky.

The ability and necessity for both women and men to become intimately connected to, know and express their soul and their self is critical in living a life in the soul's orgasm.

Sitting inside the self of the goddess is dwelling within the holy of holies, the temple within. The Goddess in her many guises and stories, may also, for some contemporary women, function as the Self.

Persephone saw this, she heard her call to go down, to help souls transition, for transformation to occur she followed her insightful realms of presence and strength, sacrificing nothing as all was in perfect divine order. She was answering her call, to serve, as she was gifted with the blessing of healing suffering through ritual of the dead, through the proper ritual, souls were able to cross over, in a peaceful way, calling forth the power in ritual and in compassion.

I went into the depths of the underworld once again.

Part Two

Naked Skin

So, what made you decide to start exotic dancing?

I really do not have an answer to that, just another job I say,

after being asked that question often. "How long have you

been here?", is always the opening one liner as I am a newbie

at the club. Three weeks I say or 3 days. They flinch in

incredulity, I don't believe that they cringe. Only one customer

laced with black diamond earrings says I believe it cause of the

way you dance. He was interested in "dating" me on my third

day. Oh yes, that was a winning comment for sure. Men, are

arrogantly a strange breed. I come up to the disc jockey booth and say men are truly pigs, and they all gather here… the disc jockey replies, yes this is their watering hole.

More like sharks really. The dancers walking around on dancer's row, are the plastic pink flamingos. Pecking at each other in a condensed natural habitat called the aquarium. Survival of the fittest rocks the mantle as rule. If one of the new and shy flamingo dancers starts flaunting her wares in such a way that threatens another, a fight ensues.

My first day on the job, my little initiation took place, they decided to give me $10 to give a guy a lap dance. Turns out it was one of the bouncers, doorkeepers, which no one does. I later found out, deathly embarrassed and then steaming with anger.

The dancer says, I don't dance with the doorkeepers around here, okay, she put me under the bus from day one. Female

Shark. I decided to pull her in, and my enemies, I apologized to her for getting angry while she was letting her urine out, she could not believe her ears, and became a "club" friend for life from that point forth. She had my back, if there was such a thing from then on.

I became a better person, after my very successful dancing stint. One thing is for sure, I learned to bite my lip, to keep my job. One that I was constantly fighting to keep. There were obstacles at every turn, people trying to take me down. From managers, to doormen, vehicles and messengers from the dark side, that saw my light as a threat. One day in the locker room I hear a man's voice, walk in. A thunderbolt of fear rushes through my body, backstage, safe, vulnerable, naked, changing, in a little thong, he orders, commands me at attention to bend over for him, What the hell are you wearing he shouts in form of everyone in the locker room? He was the one who hired me, and the owner of the club's son. Bald and disgusting, he was the one who hired me. It was the most mortifying moment until that point, I had ever had, I fought back the tears and bit my lip, it was like someone trying to rape you, fuck you, humiliate you, push you as far as you would go.

I prayed he would be sent away. Later that week, he was.

Word on the street was that he raped a young new girl, got her drunk, and raped her in the back of his car. It was all on video. What was he thinking?

He was gone. Thank GOD.

There were others trying to take down the tiara I

had acquired, they wanted to strip me from my

crown.

Control,

Self-control.

A playground for refining the way your animal

soul needs to be tamed for higher purpose.

Female Trophy

So you will wear your favorite costume

Rotate upon a pedestal

While I look upon you

Stare

Tell your story

Oops, I mean sell your story

Your naked body, in detail

"I do beautiful work"

Get a break every 15 minutes

We may call you

Rebecca.

Taken, with your permission

A snapshot of your soul

Your body that is

Your mind, your vision

Your heart, standing upon a pedestal of

Light, and dark

Detailing where you have been, the lines around the fold of

your eyes and lips

Up and down there

Those pictures will only be for us

I will give you a document

A document validating

The perversion of long ago

The pictures that were taken

The way I made you pose

Half naked

Love was the pay, I gave you

That was supposed to be enough

The love you stole and gave back to me in pieces

On laminated paper.

SO, you have anything against posing in the nude? I had no choice then...

To rotate and spin in my own blood, as my soul

left, although, now that the choice is mine,

I spit at, turned down, and leave your proposal,

grateful that my betrayal ends here, with my own voice,

on laminated paper.

Giving Away

As starting fresh

Fish

Smell

Anew

Energy

Exploring new realms of interconnected beings

Living the life of a simpleton

See what comes up next

So grateful to have been in partnership

With you

To prepare for the depths of digging deep

Demons uncovered, layers revealed in the mystery mystique

An open book sets the stage as we set our sights higher

Learning lessons of

Holding onto our skins more important than

Allowing scraping pulling them off?

Those masks that wear so thin

In disguise we wear them

Seek to please ourselves

How do we look

What color are thine eyes

In my gaze

Headstrong

Nails done heels worn

Lipstick stuck

Breaths of fresh air

Invite you into, to peek

Inside of the window

The light inside of the moving clouds moving, spinning

Now calm and ready to be graceful not only on the dance floor.

You prepared as you will be, recreating this life

On your journey inward and outward to landscapes

Readily carved.

You will know when you reach your destination and

Will know with whom to carve out your new lines together.

The sculptor, the seeker, the tumbleweed meeper.

You will both know when your faces meet.

Two willows intertwined forever.

1000 rejections underneath the sea, of sharks sometimes I think I want to be the shark instead of the flamingo. The bowl is the club, the strip club. When I leave with loads of green in my pocket, I seem to feel worthy, shining, special. Someone enjoyed my attention, even if it was with my clothes off.

I swim around as the shark and not the sweet flamingo, and no one opens their mouth to chew. Sounds like I have been saved although in this microcosm of the macro world, it is the way of survival.

Sometimes slow, always changing.

Psychic Space.

Went to the strip club the other night to watch and be the customer. It seemed I enjoyed the other role better. The attacker, the watcher instead of the one being watched. I am still the flamingo trying to be the shark, although no one wanted to eat the flamingo trying to be the shark.

You have to be the hunter and quickly surrender often even after 1000 rejections. Come, come whomever you are and place yourself down in front of a shark.

Tantra is the art of embodied spirituality. The bodies spiritual knowing of freedom and ecstasy. The creative exploration of sexual freedom is the exploration of your energy body healing itself. Cultivating, activating the bodies joy is a reunion of inner spirals of engagement and integration of immanent and transcendent energies. A full chakra spirituality is one that embraces all centers of our generative Spirit. While embracing the fullness of human experience one seeks to maintain awareness and grounding while surrendering to the senses and where they want to take us. Allowing them to take us on a journey. Onto and into the spaceship of another and the merging of both ships taking off into space, timeless, and eternal. Allowing the emergence of tasting blissful paradise, the art of taking our time to just be, here, while traveling through multiple dimensions of millennia.

Bodily sensations are foundational stepping-stones in the embodied transformation of spirit's creative energies through each human life.

Named Naked No More

As Marilyn Monroe

We revealed all to you

Naked on the stage of your life

Cried out our painful wounds

As part of our heart

Wanted you to wipe the scar tissue clean

Leave the stains of dried blood on your couch

In your bed, we felt abandoned

Abandoned our only truth

In the heat of the moment

That was cold

No fire

Passion only did what we thought was our illusion

of you

Wanted me to do

What did we want to do-we knew

Forgot all about the voice that was heard today

Today was the victory of courage of our heart's

longing

To be heard, honored and respected in the face

of fear

The repercussions bend over backwards

Forwards forever hindering success no more

As women, partners, soul mothers

Calling forth the sleeping wisdom

Hidden in mother's breast milk

The nourishment we all to give to ourselves

Full with dignity and pride to be women

In our day

All the days to come

As an extraordinary contemporary Demeter, Aphrodite and Persephone, Marilyn Monroe was the sexualized, idealized, image of the Goddess. She represents all women who are priestesses of Venus, Aphrodite, Persephone, and Demeter, searching for the ability to express and reclaim a sense of self, recovering the beauty of soul and sensual pleasures inherent in life itself.

Modern Day Transmission

Priestess to Priestess

I have chosen to state my vow to another soul.

I vow to be true to the goddess I am

I am, I am the goddess I am

She hears, honors and accepts my truth

I bow in honor of our oneness and grace

Gazing in her eyes, intimacy of knowing far

beyond the

Present moment

Holding space for all to be seen and heard.

Building community supporting healing

transformation

Invoking our ancestors, the four directions

Paying homage to the aspect She embodies

within us,

A rose

A token of her our kind birth, the vow to start

anew

A token of what has been spoken

Clenched in my hand I pray it to be so

Oh holy circle of sacred sister dance, spirit and

word

Bless us now; be here now, for we are clean and

pure

We enter the gates of the Mysteries:

I have chosen you Hygieia, for you are the mistress of

healing, the moon goddess of revelation, of mystery, the snake

we have heard and seen in our dreams. The snake of healing

that rests on my neck, giving me the message of my true

calling. The burning question answered, mark of the goddess.

Minoan temple high priestess, as was my charge then...

Atlantis remembered.

Emerging...

Wake up Wake up! Wherever you are!

I am here; I am here, to awaken souls

Your soul this moment

Awakening the secrets held in the soul through ritual, the Eleusinian mysteries were held in the highest of secrecies. Your secrets define who you are, if this is so, the Initiates of the Mysteries were ones of a sexual and sensual nature. They were a vehicle to embody and be embodied by the spirit goddesses Demeter and Persephone, creating a space for their emergence. The intermingling and mix of the deity, Spirit and the human initiates was the veil behind the secrets the mysteries held sacred. The veil came down for nine days, where there was no separation between the worlds. Souls were able to merge with deity and other souls, and be fully seen. The eyes were awakened to the heart that always feels the great mother presence.

They shaved my hair and let my glasses fall to the floor, they kicked and gagged my sister, who had amnesia and could not remember to salute them. They took us side by side and emptied their trash, our bodies, onto the conveyor belt of trains that lined the cities railways. She curled up next to me and closed her eyes and began to forget about a life she once knew. A life that I once knew, that was on it's way out of view, as the trees and buildings that were familiar were left behind, with the mixed sounds of muffled cries and eerie silence began to envelop us, as we headed towards our destination.

These memories live within the first hours of the first days when all was amidst chaos and confusion, but the soul knew, our destination was to be final. I hear the cold wind whipping across the field, before my skin grew cold and my heart numb. It did not take long, the people on the train began to wither and I began to wonder how people became dying flowers, who became merely numbers, to humiliate, beat and kick around.

We lost our identity when we were stripped; of everything. One thing we held in tact was our memories. Those who held on to them were those who assembled the morsels of love they once knew, as the morsels of bread and water were fed to them, remembering to return to the love that once was.

The soul remembers when she was a girl, before all was taken, before all was turned into a living hell. She had blond hair and blue eyes and looked like the other girls in her class. She wore a uniform and spoke French. She played outside until it was dark, and knew the joys of laughter. She began to wander the streets alone in her mind, before bed, and would often wonder what the world out there beyond the safety of her house gate held. She wondered what her destiny was and where her life would take her.

She often dressed in her mother's clothes, and placed all of her stuffed animals on a train made of chairs she would place them in. She was the leader, and danced around the space, creating an image that would be replayed, and come to haunt her dreams, with her as one of the animals, the leaders outside, blowing the whistle for the train to move forward. The vehicle that moved us closer towards our destiny would always be remembered.

Memory lives in a fish bowl of time, curling in and around the waves of decision. The realm of discernment came clear one morning as I was dressing my infant daughter, Pnina. She wiggled and let me know we were not in the throws and chambers of war. She glistened of goodness, hope, and love. Were those memories gone? Would they lie dormant only to awake and rise to torment my dreams?

It was a new time in an old familiar place. The gates that were used to lock us in our own skin and cells of denial were our new walls. The streets were the same gravel filled streets; dirt paved our way each morning. The windows they looked inside when we were exchanging vows, fogged at the sight of him. He was a soldier, a brave, handsome, soldier that asked for my hand, I agreed. He had the freedom to look and act as he pleased before they came. It was 1939, in a small town bordering Romania.

The country or the person is seen, as outside of them, the scapegoat if you will, imbuing terror with meaning it does not have. A mythic reality is carried out in order for another to cleanse themselves from their own darkness, their own perversion, weakness, powerlessness, and violent hatred of self. They then rob others of what they feel is desperately missing in their own lives.

In the beginning, war looks and feels like love. Unlike love, it gives nothing in return but an ever-deepening dependence like all narcotics, on the road to self-destruction. Finally, one ingests war to remain numb.

For survivors of childhood abuse or sexual trauma, this may show up as an addiction to the illusion of love. What looks like love addiction is ingesting sexual acts to remain numb, and re-experience an act that has been repressed and desperately yearns to resurface.

Ultimately, it is the reclaiming of self that was stripped -- the soul that left the body. Remembering the body. Coming back into a body that was unsafe. War being raged on the body. Killing the soul.

.

The moral void is revealed, when life is worth nothing and death means everything.

A nation is not conquered until the hearts of its women are on the ground. Then it is done. No matter how brave its warriors or how strong its weapons. Where shall women fall, as they birth the men that kill them, the men that fear them, and allow themselves to hate their birth, their femininity, sensuality, and softness?

How does creation birth such evil and such grace? The cyclical cycle of death and rebirth, match amongst the rotation of the sun and the moon.

Bravery, courage...what makes a heart brave? I hear the announcement on the radio, a letter in my mailbox. The comfort women of Korea; how were they used and disposed of? Their testimony is coming forward.

The Silence has Broken

The majority of the women, who provided sex for Japanese soldiers, forcibly taken from their families or were recruited deceptively. Sometimes family members were beaten or killed if they tried to rescue the women, most in their teens. Once the women arrived at the comfort station, they were forced to have sex, typically with 20 to 30 men a day. If they resisted, they were beaten or killed.

A majority of the 80,000 to 200,000 comfort women were from Korea, though others were recruited or kidnapped from China, the Philippines, Burma, and Indonesia. Some Japanese women who worked as prostitutes before the war also became comfort women.

How do men take their mothers, sisters, and beat them into the ground? The hearts of women are lying face down on the cold, hard, dirt, dying for giving their souls for life.

How do I connect the link of memory's chains, of events that seem to be out of order? Do we have evidence of being a victim, survivor, warrior, and priestess? Are they the same?

Who lives with the weapon of destruction inside of their belt buckle, the same weapon that is the same as creation? They are polar opposites. How do we understand, bridge and merge our polarities inside of ourselves?

The microcosm that is our body plays the movie of our akashic records in our souls. What is the link between the psyche, body, and spirit that has dissociated from society, how must we call back compassion into our lives?

Memories float in and out of a time that once was, and still lives inside of our soul. We lock ourselves prisons, to save ourselves from our very essence, our truth.

Running. Away. From. Self. The little boy or girl that was lost in a male or female body; the little boy or girl that was not seen, or heard, or taken care of; the little boy or girl that was abandoned; the little boy or girl that was hurt by his or her protectors; the little boy or girl who is now a man or a woman, lost in a big city.

Reclaiming Memory of the Soul

I once met a man with transient global amnesia, which he proudly and adamantly showed me a testament to the truth to back up his words by showing me a silver bracelet coiled around his seventy-six year old wrist. I met him at the Chat cafe, Encino, CA, which is located on the pier, on the Pacific Ocean.

We were immediately weaving a web as he told me stories, and I asked him questions, triggering his memories, allowing his soul to remember his life story.

His word, his heart in his tears fell down his cheek. He was forever indebted and grateful for the space that was created for remembrance. In his sharing, we both knew I would remember him and his story, the story of what happens when you forget, and what occurs for the soul when it is allowed to reclaim, memory, in essence the joy felt is a piece of liberation from suffering.

The Printmaker

Imprint of the souls knowing

Collective soul conscious

Community soul

Spirit served

Listening as waves of memory

Resurface to minds eye

Blessing in knowing

Touching healing hearts

The time for passing

Will come

Pain resurfacing

As all pushed down

Will come up as ancient ruins bind

The time's life eternity

Living, birthing, dying

Luminous space between the clouds

Pushing them to the side to see you

As you hear

Allowing us to see our self, our visions

Of my past, our own remembrance of soul

Rebuilding the structure for reclaiming

All that is already known

Creating space for another

Inspiring the beginnings of greatness

A good word to another

Seeing past the tears to give what you feel

Silence after speaking

Booming voice resonating

Heard-landing in a chalice

Of spirit served to thee

Holding onto eternity

By letting go of the needing to know

Sanctuary warrior fighting

For the space to be coded

Flooding

Eternal memories beyond and into

Eternal knowing

Passing in between worlds

Silently

The waves crash, the fire burns, four directions called, our ancestors walk in. By the fire, my eyes grow weak and weary, birthing new sight, as negativity releases its hold, and pain lives. In the caves, I lose my eyes in allowing my sight to deepen and go beyond, into realms where I become one with the earthen life force. The winds howl, the magic flows, as we invoke, and caress the Earth. Allow the waters to kiss our feet, and bless our blazing heart.

During a month long spiritual practice of meditating on the ocean, I have been filled with the undulations of the inherent life force and kundalini that has awakened inside of my being a few years ago. I feel the rising in awareness in the way I walk, speak, the erotic wavelike movements I feel in my body, spontaneously, as I write, or read, and am called to sing in reverence and praise of the magical mystical mother enlivened and continuously awakening in my soul body with each moment.

What is the ocean trying to tell me? What is the ocean trying to tell my body, and the soul memory it carries, like the sediments that come into the belly of the beach? What about the particles of sediments as the sparks that were dispersed when the earth shattered and broke its vessel in the seismic blow of creation?

The foam of the ocean as the seed of creation that exudes freshness of rebirthing over and again with each arousing tide of life force, the ecstatic energy found within us all.

Calling in creativity and sexuality is truly calling in the divine mother, in her gown of creation, the rising of the kundalini creates empowerment of women, and our essence, as the ocean embodies the waves that call us to move into trance dance. We weave the spiritual into the mundane, cultivating the freshness of being one with ocean air.

The healing dance of intimacy is found in the layers underneath the darkness. The unfolding of the cells filled with old news and past theories... the opening of cleansing will bring the old to pass and the new to light... this new light will awaken within us when we trust in the moment to bring us to our ultimate redemption.

With each birthing and re-birthing, each time our vessel becomes stronger. With each shattering, the mending is the unfolding into mama breath, the mother wound, womb, we long to reenter, to receive the nurturing and loving support all yearn for.

How do we honor our wound, and let go of the past, acknowledge and move on? Tell the story, allow someone to see and hear you, journal, mourn, yell, scream, dance, sing.

Let go, fall in the trust of transition, fall into the arms of the goddess of compassion. They are holding you in the wings, while you are not looking; walking you up the stairs at night holding you as you mourn your past and the losses you have endured, forgotten. For the memories you hold, you are held, and the Universe knows and feels your pain.

All is one with you, and all you have sustained. Spirit is the light carrying you, the shadow that draws you near, the wings you fly on and have always ridden, bringing you up, giving you love. Flying you to the ocean's edge and bringing you far above, into the clouds of mystery, and asks you to tell your story, his, hers, all of ours, our suffering as humans, is held by community.

To hold her in my arms, the Shechinah, dwelling within, embodied. As I held her, I felt the Mother, holding, nurturing, at one without breath, pain and channeling energetic love to my spine.

An awakening of humility born in conscious conclusion, a collision; the ambulance sounds the wave of erotic heart beats that call us to listen; to the sounds of our soul...

Sound, the gorgeous waves of our collective heart, singing to the life force beat of creation; silence sounding as one heart, as one breath of community.

The sounding was brought together as sacred union and marriage of the heart and soul. A gift of beads representing introspection and moon energy: passion, joy, balance, protection, and grounding.

Water Ceremony

Water cleanse of life, clearing the way for new

beginnings, Light.

As we walk towards the oceans roar, seeing the

vision of the ceremony ritual about to ensue,

circling the altar of self, seven times

Leaving footprints of pathways, Past

Weaving inward, inner circle

Sacred space inside

Womb life

Love

Circling inside of self, soul song pours forth,

vowing to be true to the goddess we are,

speaking gratitude to the one who has given

service

 In the name of the One, gracing our life spirit.

Another day, another time, I will meet you

In this world, we thank you

Soul love, life, Light

Peace in oneness

We offer all to the waters that come upon bare

skin

Immersed in purity

Given up to the one

Saluting thee

Journey through the tundra

The labyrinth of joy, flying, leaping over and under

Boundaries set before our eyes, hatching out of

the egg,

Wobbling forward, backward, to the side

Our path is hatching underneath our bones, our

wings begin to take shape, form

The hawk that is the raven, given its beak to

voice wisdom

In silence we dance our path

Allowing, Opening

To the circles and cycles that take us down

lifelines

Of the Dance

The darkness of the goddess, the dark mother submerged,

is our memory. The symbol of resistance of the dark mother, of the ancient grandmother stones embedded in our psyche, felt and expressed in our bodies, will persist, as she does in the present. The root memory of the goddess continues to dwell within our hearts as soul-life, swimming as we allow her to swim within our lives. It is how we wake to her beauty and reality that affects the rest of our day, our memory of then, that is now, and now that is then.

Divine Call

Running outside a hotel room in the middle of the night as the alarm bell sounded, our hearts were being pulled into our hands, we desperately ran for our lives, we were being called to the parking lot where all the hotel residents were gathered in their pajamas.

Shocked and angered to be awoken in such a manner. We rush to the doctor's office to be diagnosed, when we feel pain, our internal alarms ringing, waiting to find out what the commotion is all about. Although deep inside we know what the siren has called us for, in the middle of the night, leaping out of our beds and into the white night, to find a truth that is already known, deep within.

It may be a false alarm, or at times we watch hotel burning, having been saved, just in time, by a miracle. Do we ever take time to thank the alarm that woke up out of our slumber, or the one who rang the bell?

Always ringing, always moving, and pointing us in the right direction, if we would only but heed its call.

The process is in harnessing our inner and outer fire.

Wisdom of the Grandmother Crones

The grandmothers calling us home; They stand, unconsciously created, the phoenix arising from the ashes, the grandmothers sit in black and white, witnessing all the has come before them, broomsticks of silver and gold, cleansing, clearing, hang above magical beings of strength of frame, ancient symbols of their heritage, their identity, the inner seed that brought them to their true faith, survival, and closure from this world.

Grandmother, I see you sitting in the East, sitting in the East, full of knowledge and ancient wisdom, the Russian kerchief that graced your heads, many times protected you and saved you from harms way, underneath and above the wood panels of flowers in red and green on black, vivid and alive as you are and were, your voices handle in the candelabra, flickering flame, in red, and a mirror of self I see in you hang in red and blue. I see the crone in you, now.

In the North sits the Maiden, who is about to have her flame lit by the love that is yearning to manifest from heart's center.

She is the princess warrior, the voice among the nations, the one who holds praise and silent servitude. She is the one who calls the community together and asks, for help. She asks to be held in honor. She asks for her voice to be heard.

In the South in the West is the Mother, who offers her guidance, and counsel. She offers her wisdom, and nurturance. She comes out of her own shadow to stand in the light, offering a hand.

The Path to Soul.

How do we get to Her? How do we find Her?

We find her through finding ourselves--through experiencing the joy and ecstasy of holding all of ourselves, our emotions, in our body, becoming a lover of life, a lover in partnership with the ecstasies in this world. The dancer who has not yet danced, is the one who is waiting to walk her path, already awakened.

The body that tells truth, the truth that is the path to presence, the embodiment of Spirit is the way to Her. She is there. Awaiting Her Divine revelation in us all.

Dancing Soul

Dancing with you these past weeks has been electrifying, titillating, tantalizing, new, and unknown. Surfing a new sea, there is none to hold onto, yet the wrap is around my leg, and when I fall into the foam, the board, the foundation floats with me. I have entered the waters, the beautiful golden mist, above and below, the enlivened dance awaits...

The dance of intimacy, consciousness present in sexuality and sensuality; the ecstasy is found in this presence of the moment, where Spirit rests and is known.

Who is she that I yearn to dance with? My own inner partner is a she, the he, I have longed for, reconnection is with self.

The ability to know and be one with her, honor and love all of her, and her needs, voiced through harmonious pleasure.

How do you know the things you know?

Without freedom to live our passions we are living as slaves, and in servitude to morals and values that are not our own. We must look deep within to see a new vision of what brings us joy and peace, and work form that humble place to serve in the capacity of our soul's purpose.

That is the essence of what gives us meaning, doing the daily non routine, but instead our calling…each day imagine waking to and by your calling in this universe, that which calls your particular soul to wake and serve each day. A financial banker may have become a farmer, and is miserable with his wealth when if he followed his deepest passions he could become much wealthier, being out in the fields raising his cattle.

Love is greater than fear.

This eternal flame begins to burn when you are honoring your passion, your deepest hearts desire.

What brings a smile to your face when you think about giving to the world, when you imagine yourself bringing forth your own wisdom to enlighten and embrace humanity, or simply what brings joy to your heart and allows its petals to open? This opening of the powerful lotus heart is the seat and core center of your spiritual apparatus called knowing.

What do you know? How do you know the things you know? When we come across our own neurosis about our looks, our clothes, our cars, homes, we believe we are deriving pleasure from external sources, by receiving the "love: or approval of society, the false society.

This comes from acting, from a base animalistic level. When coming from the soul level, true pleasure comes from intimacy, platonic everyday casual interaction filled with genuine interest and care, as well as sexual intimacy which brings us to the ultimate weaving of body and soul, and essentially bringing heaven down to earth. That which we seek in material items, bigger, fancier, more seductive, is really a seduction of union.

The union of souls. This union will bring the opposing polar opposites in our bodies to integrate as one force, a powerful life force that energizes and heals our bodies, our souls, and the world.

Embodying the Divine

All who find happiness in the world have done so by wishing for the

happiness of many others. All who find unhappiness in this world

have done so by aiming just for their own happiness

What makes up the landscape of a soul who has not been

allowed to exhale their story? It is one of utter disillusionment

with life, and it's purpose. What becomes of a heart that has

not seen or understood the sunset? It is a heart that beats and

bleeds white; of not knowing; the white of purity, the blood of

surrender--the ego.

What makes up the heart of someone who has risked

everything to speak their truth and BE their calling? What

becomes of the heart that dies trying to awaken, and speak again? What happens to the womb of that heart, as it holds creation and wonder of life itself?

Oh how I yearn, to touch thee, the creatrix, the womb, the Tantric goddess that holds all of us in her earth, as she makes room for us in Hers. Oh sacred goddess you have moved aside to welcome our presence, and we come forth into being by your nurturance, your space. When we move to the side and place our ego underneath layers of pain and anguish, we allow you to enter and return to our wombs of creation.

Allow us to return to our true essence of erotic soul. The cleaving and bonding with you, the witness and desire of engaging in the depths of union and erotic bliss as a result of knowing our inner sanctum of divine feminine love; it is the cauldron for all to be born into and out *of.* The recipe for creation begins within our own bodies and minds in the preparing and clearing of the space with ingredients made and mixed with care, as we follow the way, we create ceremony of the soul.

What a day to remember how precious life is. A day to remember how sacred we are, a day to remember our inner wisdom we have acquired through trials and tribulations. A day to soothe your heart for it still bleeds red. It still wakes in the morn. It gives you the chance to relive another day as if it were for the second time; you have the choice on how you chose to live in harmony with your dragon spirit.

I am the dancer waiting to be danced. I am the dance awaiting unraveling, the unfolding of my inner sacred. My soul is the breath that yearns to be taken. The retrieval of her is the return of the soul to its body, its temple, the return of the goddess to earth.

To be known, revered, and remembered. Coming forth to honor the sacred within you, I bow and vow to honor the goddess within. My voice is your voice. Mamacita, I 'm coming home, to a place within my soul. Pachamama, I'm coming home, to a place we all know.To a place we all know.

Dragon Spirit

She breathes into your heart and takes away the pain. She strengthens your will by allowing you to believe in your inner heart's chamber, flowing and pumping with blood.

Calling of the womb: returning to the mother of your soul's heart, the blood that speaks through your veins, I remember you, queen goddess who runs through the night, the one goddess who calls me home.

Celebrating the end of suppression, disassociation, and return of ultimate humility, she runs past the gallows and onto her riverbed on roses, seeking all that she will find. In a trance, she finds her past, her present, and her future, all set before her.

The golden field of rubies is her treasure inside her heart. Opened and revealed to the few that write of her beyond the spheres of time, in this world where all rests and abounds with pleasure when she reveals herself, unravels the secret wounds that she lies in the core of. The sacred sexual wound of the second heart, the womb of the first heart, holds the blood that speaks truths and gives life, as does the second.

Opening, unraveling, in sacred robe garb, slipped on golden shoes walking quietly in the night.

You have entered the realms of the sacred, and have unlocked the key to the underworld my Queen of Sheba, queen of lights, queen of the night shades that rules Sight.

Can you help me? Can you see? Can you please the internal part of me? Oh yes, sire I can only know what beckons me to yell and scream my voice in yours oh how I yearn to touch thee. The smells of desire, the one that lights my heart on fire, you will know, you will both know and come together as one in no time at all. All is one time, for all time.

She groans from time to time. There is a time, for everything to speed up time is to play with the pencil on canvas that Spirit holds. We hold the paint that fills in the lines of our attitude, our creation is a CO-creation, what we say and how we think, our mind's eye becomes our chamber, our canvas, our sketch pad, our design. Our lives become ours; we claim them as such. We acknowledge our choice and our will to surrender to another will, Spirit, within and without. There, without knowing we will know, we will hear; we will speak, the designs of our heart.

Ceremony of Soul

Sacrificed, painted body, in preparation of the sacred revelation, of you. Erotic touch mastered needed, you are being gifted, shackled by the King, requesting your presence as his. Honored by the women worshipping you in divine contemplation, of power withheld, power, within. Fortress denied inside of the palace gates that are your throne. You reach for your scepter, and allow the flowing inwards towards your bloodline revealed in the right time.

Carried, swept away by time travel, in a chariot carried by hidden men, the chariot I have been riding in, in this world, carried over from the past. Which do I now chose? Has one already chosen me?

The walls are wailing; they hold the pain of the goddess, exiled, Her cellular memory, of all of those who have passed, all the women who have been silenced and banished from their hearts and bodies.

For all the men and women who have been invisible; all the curses bestowed for our inner fires burning, for our creation story, and the myth of our destruction. We are givers, transformers of life, death, and midwives of rebirth. The silence of the darkness vilifies the only mystery known to humankind, the desperado dance chamber of the inner heart, where do they open and flow from? What is their lifeblood path?

Delving deeper into you, I see my own mirror, so beautiful, and full, my cup is no longer empty, my reflection is no longer dull, the veil is now transparent. I scream my own light of beauty from beyond. Distraction the veils, protection, honor, and artistry we're coming home-to the heart of my soul.

The raven lands on the shores of the sand, on the rock, by my side, the only one calling, standing, strong, calling me home, to my heart, to my soul, as the waves crash, I know stillness.

"Where there is ecstasy, all opposites coincide, sexual communion is a way of expressing wholeness."

According to Tantric mythology, this universe is the love-play of a divine being which split itself in two, a male and a female half, so that it might know the ecstasy of love.

All men are splinters of this original god, all women of the goddess, and through their lovemaking, God experiences the rapture of reunion.

The single most revered aspect in Tantrism is Goddess Worship. The Divine is polarized into feminine and masculine, respectively called Shakti and Shiva.

In the ancient Indian temples, priests and priestesses lived and worked side by side, sometimes becoming lovers. However, in the rituals designed to celebrate God's lovemaking with the world, the priestess seems to have played a very different role than the priest. The male's job is to relate to life. The female's job is to become it. The man's function is to act. The woman's function is to be. A similar view seems to have prevailed in ancient India. Priests were defined by their actions maintaining the rituals, maintaining the temple compound, and so on. Priestesses were primarily defined by their female being, and by their knowledge of the triple mysteries of the physical body: birth, sex, and death.

With the arrival of patriarchy, the sexual customs of the priestesses contributed to their downfall. In a culture that valued female chastity and submissiveness, there was no place for these non-monogamous, proud, independent priestesses. Gradually, their tradition deteriorated, and the British eventually completed their demise by cutting off financial support to the temples, defaming the priestesses as prostitutes, and making their dances illegal, which they remained until India gained its independence in 1947.

The healing may begin when you allow your creative energy, your life force energy to flow inside of your body.

Sacred Sexuality is not about energy play or intercourse per se, but the communing or identifying with the ultimate Reality, the Divine

Many times our bodies are taken from us by force, or through violence, as a result our soul leaves the body, as the trauma is too great to bear. In the case of early childhood trauma, memories are suppressed into the unconscious mind, accessible later in life, often times by a similar, 'triggering event."

A large part of the journey of authentic knowing is the reclaiming of our bodies as temples, as strong and powerful. A deepening and surrendering to self as beautiful, graceful, and wild embodied fullness…

The journey of acceptance and essentially emerging as gratitude to being naked in the darkness, revealing our radiant light in the precious presence of the present moment.

I was blessed with a deep sensual shamanic journey, as a reflection of my past and present inner birthing and awakening. Kundalini embodied, the journey taken.

By surrendering control and giving to the process, allowing the body to feel every nuance, honor each subtle motion of the soul asking to be expressed and honored, without a definable or end goal.

This is the spontaneous ritual that brings one in touch with divinity. This is the power of movement, the power of meditation. This was the power of creation. The power we all have at any moment, to create ourselves anew, and return to our true nature our soul's inherent nature of divinity.

Calling Soul Home

The dance pours through, as the icicle melts

Ocean air.

Gliding in its fluidity

In motion, we call our soul home,

Back into our body

Where it breathes and belongs

Knowing arrival

We begin the shamanic journey,

We know has been coming

Waiting to be taken up, upon its calling

Wonder evades wisdom beyond compare.

Mindless emotion bubbles up to the surface

After having dove deep into its belly

The whale of soul memory

To renew and reclaim body knowing wisdom

Of ancient kind

We begin by pushing, all out

We begin by feeling the insides of the womb

Allowing play in its holy waters Home

Holding, immersion into self,

Oneness, present

Believe in my wholeness

We ask you to know us

We ask you to hold our being

Where we are and how we are

We ask you to believe we are with soul

Rising through my past Kundalini awakening,

Life force reawakening

Being born, giving birth to creation, to soul

initiation

To spirit life,

Loved.

In the beginning there were the waters

Climbing to scream

On top of from innards

Of clarity, of knowing

Sensing primal vitality

Born into existence

Soul.

 We are monkey.

We are the before and after.

We are the raven-hawk soaring overhead.

We are the wisdom from below.

We are bowing to immersion.

Dissolving into all we know.

Oneness.

Driving into the temple I saw him out of the corner of my eye,
straight ass, straight jacket standing there to protect, who from
whom? One thing I knew was he was watching me. How I
parked, what kind of car I drove, and yet I welcomed the gaze,
somehow. After all those years of being watched, as I ate, as I
was stared down, in the military prison that was my home. At
times, the kitchen, branded unworthy for spilling food on my
shirt, I got out of my already labeled "screamer, how did he
ever know.

It was a beautiful night, cool, clear, and perfect, and it was
Mimuna, the last night of Passover, and the electric celebration
of the Sephardi Jews. As I entered the temple, pressure for
payment and a ticket came quickly, the family atmosphere was

a bit much to bear so I stepped out onto the sidewalk, where he awaited to be entertained.

A detective, someday to become sheriff, while protecting the Jews came into dialogue with me. The attraction was intense, he could not stop bumping his finger onto my body, I told him I was never attracted to men in uniform, as some women are. I also told him that he was to stay in his circle, and not enter my space. As I lightly touched his hand with the tip of my finger he jokingly told me not to touch him, the same limit I set for others. He wanted to obey, and I felt a tension in my back and neck as I do when someone is thinking of me, or I feel something is not right. He wanted me, that night, although "we" were unavailable, to each other. Were we?

Forbidden

Playing with fire, An arm encircled

Barbed wire, Crossing the fence

Barriers, thorny, Immense

Hidden, **Deep in the forest**

Thicket, So dense, Wolf howls

Embittering echoes

Out on the prowl

Danger, Seduction

Where lethal passions lie

Slice open your heart

Let me inside

Tainted blood spills, Tiny crevices filled

Mixing, Forbidden-Touch

Ah-so hot, Soft and warm

Dignity, Pride, Stripped cut, torn

Sexual desire, Burned

On fire

We debated the true definition of victimhood. John, the

detective, spoke of personal responsibility and the difference

between coming into a parking lot and being robbed as

opposed to deciding to go to a party with a group of bikers, and being hurt as a result.

Risk-taking. I tell him of the night before. While walking down the street on fourth avenue, I glanced into a café looking space, while I was being noticed by two older biker looking men. The shorter of the two, asked me if that was a lesbian bar? I said, you think I'm a lesbian don't you? No, I am just here to check out the culture of the place." I repeat, you think I am a lesbian because I have short hair." No, he says, I enjoy lesbians, and you have a nice ass." I know I replied." He starts laughing at the fact I agree with him. He continues along with me down the street, seems harmless and sweet, he follows me into the Romanian Teahouse. Are you coming in? Do you want me to? He asks. No, I say.

Circular Face

My body

Pulsates

To the beat of the drum

His soft smooth

Rubbery hands

Glide and caress the circular face

Pulsating body

That quickens with each sensuous tap

Gearing my inner vessels to receive love

Becoming one with the forbidden

He walks in anyway, says he'll by me drink. I say I do not drink. I pick a table low to the ground with a golden covered circular top across from where the band Jamaican Trance will soon play.

His name is Simon, and he thinks I do not wear underwear, wants to know how kinky I really am, and if I will go to Mexico with him tomorrow. Mexico is not a risk I am willing to take, I say.

He says maybe I'll marry him while I am there, as my eyes do not lie, and he does not like to waste time. He says, he wasted sixteen years with someone who he found out he really did not know at all. So our thirty-second meeting has an equal chance of success, according to his calculations.

Simon tells me about when he was a boy, and about the dream he remembers since he was two or three years old. He told his mother and I the same vision, "I was on a dolly being rolled into a room with pipes on the ceiling. I saw the doors open, and felt the cold. The sheets were white, there was a bright light as I was being rolled in."

He saw me as a Madame. I thought maybe we knew each other in a past life, a gypsy life. In this lifetime he did refrigeration. Johnny Depp, and Jay Leno were among the many he knew as customers. He thought I could make money doing stand up comedy at the Improv in LA, he told me he did their refrigeration....

At the morgue…he saw the pipes that followed him in his dream, and he knew right away that he had died and came back once, twice, he said he did not buy his own ticket, and would get off when his ride was up.

He regretted not staying in Bangkok, when he was in the military. Simon lived for his daughter who broke her arm the same day he broke his leg. First broken bone for both of them. He began to tear as he told me this synchronistic story. He wished he could have prevented her from any pain.

Simon, was a Jewish man, who had seen too much, as he said. He was a man who saw inside of my eyes and soul. Although when he asked when he could see me again, I told him we were just … he finished my sentence…ships passing each other at night.

While visiting many tantric temple all the United States, I was ready to open my own. I was ready to become a Tantric Madame. No wonder the young nineteen year old woman saw me as a mother figure at the club, I had only been dancing a few months longer than her, but I was her mother's age, I was careful to keep my enemies close, but did not see any reason to make friends or reveal anything to anyone else. I did make great friends with the cook. He was always there, a rock star of sorts who was there to feed me a bit and hear some stories about what was happening, this pro ball player wanting to take me home, how I refused, and how I did not do drugs or give my phone number out for sexual favors. I gave him a bear squeeze the day I walked out, thanked him, and told him he was the best, he replied with the same. There was a mutual respect and understanding we had.

The tantric temples varied amongst each other, nothing like what I had envisioned in my first visioning back at school, in the classroom the first day of class. Yet, for modern-day standards it would do, as society did not remember the times when temples were THE place to be, go and be healed on many levels, including sexually.

Some temples were filled with younger and older women, trying to make a buck, heal themselves, all searching for god in some way or another.

The grand temples trained in, were private retreat homes in the ritziest of neighborhoods all over the country. Some had indoor pools over looking the ocean, teachers that were eighty years old, swimming nakedly in the pool while we listened and learned about connection and energy play in the wet waters of sensual play.

Eighty was the new twenty in my eyes, the energetics of the eighty year old teacher who I as praying was not going to be my partner, shocked my senses and awakened my synapses as my mind was altered after being fully aroused by his subtle, gentle, loving and very sexual nature. The way he gazed the tantric glance, and gently carried me over the waters edge. Grandfather or not, he was a master at energy. The love energy.

For in bowing to the moment at hand

We bow in to the sacred stillness of silence, and

the gratitude of awakening

Perfection of rising dawn

As the moon slides below the belt-line of the

sea…sitting…in a lotus

Opening, unfolding, the sun's rays

Beckoning towards arrival

Changing our posture in the beginning, clues us

into the ending of changing

Emptying into stillness.

Poetics: Not only a record of experience but a plea of despair:

It is not a cry for sympathy but a call for strength.

A prayer calling forth what was, and what could be, our vision, our potential. Personally, collectively, we enter into and from a vast remnant of who were then, in our former lives on this earth, and on many others

Poetry: a trace, evidence

A poem may be the only evidence that an event occurred; it exists for us as the sole trace of an occurrence.

In writing, we are able to mirror and commit to what is unfolding inside of us; it is a testimony, a witness if you will, of our own inner life. It is a way to leave a legacy behind, even in the midst of a death march, on our way to the chambers, of exiting this world in the face of fear. Many others in the Holocaust, and concentration work camps, had their soul language intermingling with their own blood, their inner knowing that their words were their last legacy.

We must go within to find our own answers. Many poets did not survive, but their works lived on, they remain with us as a witness to the dark times, politically and the nonexistent boundary of the personal was expressed and sung in their times, their personal which became communal for all. War songs of old are new as we excavate and rediscover ourselves in them.

Yearning to feel alive and know freedom from the inside; to know this body through laughter and full body orgasm, a freedom cherished. To dance into stillness until truth floods body, veins; many ways to know sacred truth.

My burning to know, to reclaim, remember, empower, and awaken my own body as spiritual and sacred in everyday living was all encompassing and overwhelming; where my own mother memories, as I peeled the inner folds of my spiritual and sensual journey, my own inner divinity was revealed.

The pubic V, the unfolding of the labia, is the unfolding of the mystery through birth, death, and rebirth, the color red ochre. The red ochre is the blood of the mystery, of sacred mother knowing. It is the essential sign of life, wisdom, and woman.

The soul is the pathway to reuniting with the divine. The living expression of an ecstatic life is one of journeying inside to receive and awaken our true voice of revelation. The true orgiastic sensation is that of coming home to divine union. These daily momentary experiences of Orgasm bring us closer to Spirit. Trance is the vehicle in which we arrive at Orgasm—a sacred way of knowing and discovering our own soul's memories, and who we truly are.

> Taking the risk of revealing the hidden within ourselves to ourselves will mean the difference between which side of the veil we live on. When we venture to journey into other realms of space and time, we journey to and through Orgasmic Sight of knowledge, of Divinity. Our

craving goes unheard and unanswered when we seek
spiritual, physical, emotional fulfillment, outside of
ourselves.

The transformation of the earth is reflective of the
psyche. There is a Kabbalistic saying, "As above, so below."
The heavens and the earth, mind, body, and spirit. I was
privileged to spend ten days on a farm, witnessing life, death,
transition, and transformation of the land, and our own inner
landscapes, including the birthing pangs of a pregnant mother
goat, who gave birth to four kids, one who was nursed, yet it
was her time to pass. The mysteries, were ever present,
serving as a mirror to our inner psyche, our interaction with the
external world, with our own Buddha nature, ever present.

The messages of body ecosystems, will deteriorate if they are neglected, their resources not renewed and nourished. As is the forest that was nurtured, after a storming wildfire that ravaged the farm, the only thing that kept it all alive, is the faith of the people tending the land, loving the land, as if it was a part of themselves' part of their body, part of their souls.

The land as a metaphor for the body, the body of mother earth, our bodies, ourselves. What is she trying to tell us? How do we bring heaven and earth together inside of ourselves and around us? How do we bring heaven down to earth?

Our bodies are our alchemical vessels for the transformation of the soul. The body has a, " Purpose of conversion and transformation, in turn promoting a turning away or letting go of the feelings or memories that no longer serve us or allow us to dwell in fullness and joy." This notion goes hand in hand with the ethics and maxims of permaculture, "Giving away surplus," that which we do not need.

The search for material wealth, fame, and power, as opposed to living with and taking care of the earth, while nourishing each other. These are the ethics of building a community container to support the multiplication of all ecosystems on the earth, cooperating while valuing the gifts and contributions of all people present.   This is the idea of going into the center of the earth, to visit our interior, the depths of our own unconscious, as well as the externals world's earth psyche.

The serpent and the lizard exemplify alchemy, and the alchemical process of transformation and renewal. The serpent eats it's own tail, giving death and birth to itself.

Macrocosm. Microcosm.

How do we make the impossible, possible, the alchemists stone, or kidney stone, appear and disappear? To make a biological stone disappear with love and prayer, and intention? Is this medically possible? This is the gold we must look towards, this is the gold that beseeches us to take heed. The edge of this communion of dancing flames, asks us to transform sickness into health. It asks us to allow for the communion of body, mind, and spirit.

How is the inner and outer gold revealed in the transformation of soul? Sources of light and dark intercede on behalf of the person, and transform our consciousness. The language of the psyche is consciousness, and intuition the language of the soul. The meeting and merging of these two powerful forces come forth in unification of intelligence and earth.

The denial that happens when garbage is placed in garbage dumps all across America, and elsewhere, a reflection of not being able to deal with our own personal unconscious. We must allow for the unearthed stories, pain and trauma to surface, to provide a space for the shadow, the dark energy of the cosmos, in our psyche, and soul.

So the pieces and processes of the uncovered layers of the demonic, of the shadow lie in waiting to come out from behind the veils of illusion, allowing us too see the non-duality of existence. All states are part of our dualistic, ego nature in that they are bound by the law of opposites, which states that everything in time will turn into its opposite.

We were able to plant a sacred grove of trees, while giving blessings. This opened my eyes and mind, to the mirroring of the planting as giving back to the earth so she may give to us. The elements of fertility were calling forth for us to bear witness to the birth giving cycle again. From the myth of Inanna, as in the art of Paleolithic and Neolithic times, the language that combines sexual imagery with images of the earth's fecund beauty.

Inanna's Hymn:

He has sprouted; he has burgeoned.

He is lettuce planted by the water

He is the one my womb loves best

My eager impetuous caresser of the navel

My caresser of soft thighs

He is the one my womb loves best

He is the lettuce planted by water

Her lover Dumuzi answers her, allowing us to see the

sexual rites as going back to agrarian culture.

Oh, Lady, your breast is your field

Inanna, your breast is your field

Your broad field pours out plants

Your broad field pours out grain

I just don't think you can give me what I want and need. Well, that's a first, when I thought he was my cheesecake fantasy, when the fantasy was illusion, and of course nothing it was cracked up to be.

Wow. The pop art of Princess Diana as a Geisha spells more than lyrical prose when I think of it.

Healing Strength. Celibacy.

Cursory remarks.

Remains in pores of soreness. Caring for rain, impressing onto my skin tones

Brown of orange. Strangeness. Celibacy was one answer. Burning Heart, Wounded Womb. The burning heart, has something to tell you, before we become closer.

Burning.

The burning of the wounding. The eyes of fire that burn has now spread.

It burns when I think of the branding I envisioned, the scar left by betrayal of past and present. Burning. With the fire of truth and lies. With the barbed wire that keeps away desire. Burning to be free, and swim in love. Burning to fly away with the dove. I sit in circle and chant. The praise of the green Tara, the Buddhist Goddess. Who claims the responsibility of the healing of all beings in suffering. Om Tara To tare soha. My heart sings in prayer, my most soulful voice. As what feels to be an ocean of tears come down. Heavy on the left side of my cheek wrapped in one. I feel the tear as a bubble of pain brought back and remembered. As I share this past and present pain with you I fear your response, the wave of fear pulsating in my heart womb in the throws of sadness....and can

only trust that in this moment

The angels have deemed our union.

Back Door

I was your escape, your back door. Is there a policy on that?

Creating boundaries and intentions to fill your inner hole, you

saw my incision, you saw my own hole, being sewn, You

chased to re-open my wounds, and yes, my hole. CO-

dependence is using another

as a tool or plaything, a toy, this is truly the simple part. You

write it's so simple, we were just drawn to each other, then you

made a choice to pursue me, Knowing how unavailable you

were, and how it was against my deepest beliefs, to be with a

married man, same as the first dance, a betrayal of all involved,

you felt it and knew it all along.

Betrayal can only happen when we betray our own inner voice,

period. The story of using and being used has followed me

because it has been true> Starting in childhood, and now ending, I believe I was with you to close my hole once and for all, and become WHOLE.

I believe I was with you to remember my own beauty, the one you really did not see,

the one that was lurking underneath you trying to fill your own soul, I believe I was with you to understand and experience what it is like for other women and men from both sides of the spectrum. The magic was an enchantment of soul knowing from the past

that was not a dance for this lifetime. When truth and illusion merge to form reality

each moment fades Into black bleeding white. Heavy river rain, lovesick standing on the shores of ego deception, seeing out of three eyes, movie screen goes blank

As the head the projector of projection, buried alive in the forest trees.

Where love overflows was not inverted and became the noose, around the neck of the soldier who went to save her amidst the flames. He became weak and impotent afraid of the roaring fire within his heart facing death he found his home.

Amongst the waking halfsies who dug their way through, the dark tunnel by speaking in whispers and hearing in ghostly tongues in languages he does not know he hears, himself as he scrapes the earthen walls....Transforming pain into production creating, manifesting your own destiny touching the page with your pen. To be surprised at what will come, to have faith in yourself is to love yourself-deeply—to caress the heart and mind that carry you not any other, You carry yourself within, all that lurks inside your shadow. This time is almost over and you will look back on it, and see its wisdom flow.

That put me through ten wringers

Dried me out only to renew

I do feel, I have been in a tunnel

I have just gotten over the hard part

Although it is still rocky

 I see the way out

Purity of Loving. Never having known its shores or core, I
rejected the only ones I was given. Twice. Adam and Aaron.
They have both come to me in dreams reminding me of what is
true, and what is possible. Reminding me not to give up and
hope.

Hope for what is pure and true, hope for love.

For being loved.

Hope for remembering my inner purity.

Then I realized he had nothing more to offer me. The stock broker, multimillionaire who used, abused and threw me away when he was done, was the one I had put my life on hold for. He was the one I yearned for, prayed for him to realize he loved me. Wanted me. Wanted to marry me and build a family. It was a very long and painful illusion. I was Suzy side helpings, an afterthought he flew to Albuquerque, New Mexico to be with. He knew what he was doing and did not let me know the time of his arrival, treating me less than. He said he was a slave to the business, while I realized I am no longer enslaved to him. My heart is done breaking for William Isaacson.

These were all faces of the same evil, the devil that would not sleep alone, and the one who always did.

Gypsy Caravan

My eyes squeal to run the other way

My heart winces in pain to stay

Leaving the aftertaste of vomit in my belly

There is no more to say to the path and mistakes I have led

Left behind in my wake

The quiet has soothed my souls yearning for solace

This nights breath gasps for air

Heart wrenches out of reach

Wallet spilled empty

Taken I have given

Nothing left nothing left

In this gypsy's caravan.

The system has been betrayed

I stayed for the merry go round

I rode on the horse and buggy

In those days

I was the beauty queen

The caravan has taken me in

With its golden shimmer and color of night

I choose myself.

I honor myself by giving to myself first, in other words loving myself as a primary responsibility to humanity. To be on your path, being focused on your honor and care of self, so that you may give to another. That person will earn your trust. As you have infinite trust in the Universe to bring you exactly what you need in the right time and at every time. This includes challenges, which are truly opportunities for self-growth and development.

This trust in spirit and in your inner wisdom, the intuition, body wisdom and the psychic or soul wisdom, you open the gates to enlightenment by turning the mirror of holiness and infinity inward. Infinite possibilities arise when you bring your highest vision of yourself forward.

Your highest self is hiding underneath the outer folds, the outer knowing or knowledge we have acquired through academics, truly comes into manifestation, or birthed into reality is when the trust is there for the unfolding of the inner folds, in other words the body wisdom of intuition, and soul wisdom, or psychic ability, to become electrified through the chakra system, of energy centers, which are activated through the epicenter of the orgasmic reality that is the core of our universe, the earth, mother earth, in our bodies.

The epicenter of our body vibrates in praise and exaltation to what is holy and all encompassing, which is the highest pulsation of love and light as the emanation of ecstatic reverence for the mother. Our mother, our womb, mother earth, the all encompassing compassion and wisdom that takes the form of divine embrace in a coupling of divine pairs. The sacred masculine brings heaven down to earth through the sacred feminine. She is the embodiment of all infinite form, while he is the messenger, the deliverer of information.

When we access the information that brings us joy, happiness, and truth, our truth, the universal truth, all shadows become equal as we move and embrace the otherness inside of ourselves. The foreign bodies of war and deceit of betrayal and wounding, have come to teach us to embrace all inside our beings. Loving and forgiving all that has occurred, all those who have touched our lives in any and every way. Opening to the understanding that all the particles we carry have made us who we are. While aware of this, our journey is to bring deep cleansing healing to these planets we live in called cell bodies, light bodies, the energy body that makes up who we are. When we dive into our energy bodies, we dive into the softness of mother. The softness of a compassionate all knowing heart. The capacity of the all-knowing heart to bridge the worlds of creation, emanation, through purity and freedom of action. This ultimate integrity is the alignment and integration of our highest selves and our root chakra self. Meaning the one who knows by seeing inside and feeling on the inside. Power flows to where our attention goes. We manifest by placing all of our energies, mind, body, and soul, on what we desire. The knowledge of desire comes to us in the form of prayer. The messages come through our prayer and or meditation for the highest good of all involved.

By trusting that our wisdom comes from the inside, from our sacred vessels of light we ensure self-sovereignty and faith in the universal energy and spirit that makes us who we are.

Arousing a woman's internal fire…is the woman becoming her immortal self, it is the inviting and the igniting of youth and vitality.

In a world where a man fears his desire for multiple partners and fears societal judgment around the myth of the immorality of desire. Desiring too much sex, or as many partners.

What shall we make of this flamboyant discussion?

Men that are committed to supporting the sacred feminine in her own power.

Bring the divine feminine aspect of a man's being into awareness through cultivating the eternal nature of his soul.

The semen is mothers milk, and mother's milk is the semen, the all nourishing manna that both feeds our hunger and soothes our longing for something greater, something outside of ourselves we are in union with, and connected to, something that we know gives us the desired feeling of wholeness and health. We know by being bathed in the spiritual sensuality of this soft, gentle, liquid of love that we have come home. To the womb of the universe that always hold us safe, protected, and worthy of the love it holds.

Know that there is a place in all of us that remains pure, the holy of holies, our inner sanctum. It is the place that has never been touched, abused, or degraded, raped, or abandoned, but honored for all of who we are.

Revisiting this truth as I journeyed into a love temple of women in Sacramento, California. Here, a group of women meditated and gazed into each others eyes, while holding the intention of seeing the woman in front of them as an embodiment of pure love and light. The goddess danced, embodied. The fully embodied women set the intention set for the evening ...embodied fullness! Radiating the reflection of a loving community, these women were seeking connection and healing, after a lifetime of separation, disconnectedness, and abandonment from true Self.

The piercing wail of the goddess to come home to her own heart inside of all of us: The essence of soul is the ecstasy born out of reverence for creation the goddess, our own personal divine feminine heart in exile, is the soul in exile.

Remembering the sacred circle of women, joining in, becoming the ancient embodiment of wisdom, in going back to our roots, to the land of our people, to reclaim our heritage and sacred lineage. To learn what it means to be a woman, of wisdom, to sink into the depths of mystic ecstasy of tradition and its esoteric wisdom. I now reclaim the goddess that has been buried, lost, and forgotten--the holding of the memories in our body and the grief that comes from the patriarchal worldview of war and violence, the suppression of inner knowing and intuition.

We bring our inner beauty to the depths of darkness only to awaken the light within us, burning love.

The love that is in our hearts is the greatest force we have to move in tune with…what do our hearts say…what is our greatest longing…what do we ache for?

I touch when I am moved from the inside to do so. I wake to the morning glow after the rains have fallen. I remember our journey, many lifetimes, present.

The heart of woman's lost spiritual legacy, the most powerful traditions of the ancient world came from the frame drum. The drum was the means our ancestors used to summon the Goddess, and was the instrument through which she spoke. The drumming priestess was the intermediary between the divine and human realms. She was the voice of the community, and the goddess herself through the drum beat, the heart beat of the goddess. She was the summoner, the transformer, bringing, invoking, and transmitting divine energy to the community.

As the bullfrogs have come out to sing their song in the rain, until the wee hours of the night, I lie awake listening, trying to make sense of their croaking. Listening to how their collective voices may be my teacher. My initial reaction was hoping for the frogs to become silent, as they do not sing the sounds of nightingales, singing comforting and soothing ballads. They shriek throughout the night, as if there were an earthquake coming. Although this is their voice, their way of communicating earthquakes and celebrations to each other, warning all around them of the burning in their hearts, coming forth in a different language, in the form others may think is unpleasant, and or quite disturbing.

The unintentional aspects of the music we make, the unwanted note, the cracked voice, the strange croaking sound we try to avoid, contains more wisdom than we think. This is a metaphor for life's innocuous unplanned moments that may look like disaster, paint splashed on a canvas, yet reveals the most beautiful picture.

In essence, we must awaken to the right and need of all sounds and languages to be heard. A safe space is begging to be created, especially in educational settings where diversity of voice is the Buddha, the goddess, divinity, speaking through all of us. Now is the time to remember to speak your truth and honor those who have the courage to do so, in such a way for other brothers and sisters to be held in theirs. This is a charge to all of us to remain true to our inner spirit, and to honor love's voice, by committing to sacred listening. In the act of hearing, you experience a part of the creation that made you, something that has been alive from the very beginning, something you can't quite remember. The music allows you to witness the actual spark.

When voice and space for authentic self-expression are taken away, we lose our knowledge of and sense of self. The true self disappears and is replaced by another's concept or idea of who we are and how we should be. The soul-print inside of the seed is not allowed to reveal itself, it is lambasted with sauce of a different flavor, one that is not our own. We then become the roasted chicken, one who has been killed for the sake of another's appetite as they fill their own hunger needs. Whether of ego or of physical nourishment, this is not the way of the tiger.

She remembers a time when masculine and feminine were honored and revered as such, when bodies were held as holy and sacred vessels. The depth of a woman resides in the earth, where earth meets breath, and voice meets sound, sacred sounding, grounding. Entering the pulsating womb space, the earth awaits your return to her as you lie in her arms, allow yourself to sink into her depths, soaking inside of her womb, you begin to remember Love's voice.

Each tone becomes a metaphor for the moment of your origin. You never lose it, the music says, no matter how long it's been gone. It's here now, here, now.

To help you remember yourself…

Remember when you were other?

Remember when your voice was silenced?

Remember when you were blamed for being the victim of violence?

Remember when you felt the web? When you felt your soul as another?

Remember when you had voice and freedom to speak your truth?

Remember when you poured your heart out in song, and it was honored as such.

Sacred Sound healing ecstasy?

All shamans have several power songs because the vibration of the notes in the voice and in the fourth chakra of the throat stimulates sympathetic vibrations in the universe to respond. I have had the honor of studying with honored shamans, and with two sound shamans in particular. My friend Joy brought forth sounds from her soul that were shocking and placed me at awe at what a human voice may channel with the ability to heal.

Everything is connected. What you put out comes back to you. When a butterfly flutters his wings in Cost Rica the winds of Africa are stirred. When a sound is offered, the universe responds.

Later that summer, I heard my own power song, as part of meeting a female shaman trained by a renowned Pomo shaman. Power songs are said to be used in preparation for journeying, healing, offering Reiki, praying, grounding, for protection, for celebration, for solace, anytime one wants to connect with the universe in this very special way,

Journeying

 Into depths of field

Running from your own inner illusion

Brought present

In one direction

Being moved in another

For a new dream

Bless Creation

The circle holds the space for your depth of

exploration

The witness holds the space for the sacred

presence Revealing love

To you, from within

What is your sacred story?

The story woven

Emerging

Spanning realms, shamanic journey

Led by inner source Divine light

Through the tunnel

 Birth, life, sexuality, death rebirth

Presence

SANCTIFY birthing of self,

Rebirthing oneness of being

 In the womb

Darkness, swimming

See the light, and remember

Kicking, pushing

Awakening

 Breath

Kundalini

Life force rising

Giving birth

Rebirth of Self

Unfolding

Journey taken

Found

Dissolving into waves of greatness

Our love was yesterday's death.

The story of Changing Woman's arrival onto earth is parallel

to the creation of the earth and the struggle find ourselves, and

our connection with Spirit throughout our lives. To relocate our cord of connection during the dark cloud, when we are feeling isolated, upon a mountain peak, when thunder and lightning surround us, yet if we surrender to the mystery of why and how we find ourselves in a particular land, and place, and bow to the rain and its rainbows, allowing for the magic and mystery to reveal herself to us, we align our mind, body, and soul with the essence and energies of the Universe.

Changing woman is found in her deep strength, yet in her profound humility. From the hidden she is revealed, from the darkness, a golden light emerges. She is a transformer of power, and the mundane to sacred. She is the one inside of us, that is independent, and capable, the one, who stands strong and firm amidst the chaos. She is the one who believes in us, in the eye of the storm, we have emerged. The song that yearns to be shared, its power heard.

Let us remember how some of the most important aspects of sacred living revolve around, ritual, community, and healing that ritual brings. The importance of ritual and healing in community and the teaching of ceremony and ritual, so that one may begin the healing and initiation process. Thereby, discovering the brilliance and gifts within themselves, and finding life's and their own true purpose. This initiation process may be the disease and it's healing.

May those from under our feet

Breathe the warmth of community unto us

So that the peace we seek

Mounts our bodies and sits on the chairs of our hearts,

Sprinkling love and joy all around.

I believe that everyone is born with a purpose, and this purpose must be known to ensure an integrated way of living. People ignorant of their purpose are like ships adrift in a hostile sea. They are circling around. As a result, tribal practices emphasize the discovery before birth, the business of the soul that has come into the world. Many times a person must go through the excruciatingly painful journey of an illness, a loss of a child, spouse, severe childhood trauma, to attain a deep soulful passage to his or her own soul purpose. A person's purpose is embodied in their name, thus constituting an inseparable reminder of why the person walks here with us in the world. Welcoming the strange, is a tradition well-kept by the Jewish holiday of Passover, in traditional Jewish observance. As a stranger to many lands, countries, and cultures, the question of 'Where are you from?' is a question that has followed in all places, having felt the push to avoid and skirted this question, always feeling from another land.

Many times, my travels abroad, and in the United States, have carried my being to feel and know the land. It is a reciprocal relationship. When I think of Native, I think of the land. This past summer I had my second stint in the corporate world, and my last customer was an American Indian man working in politics, with a long black ponytail. We sat down and spoke about spirituality, Native American Spirituality, my roots and experience of the Jewish tradition, and how the two were connected. He spoke of InDios: Meaning "In God" to dwell inside of Spirit. When I think of Native American I think of Spirit, being with and of Spirit. It is being connected to the land, Divinity, the Buddha, goddess nature, that is the knowing of the inner soul voyage. The soul that knows how to drum, how to sing Native chants, the soul that knows how to heal in a way that is ancient, that comes from many a life time ago, when natives were shamans and shamans were natives, ancient, holy, and often times were women.

When I think of the word Native, I think of my face in the mirror on all of those paintings in those frames, in the hallways of those hotels in the desert, in the town of, Santa Fe, Mexico, they knew me, I knew them, they were there, I was them, I remembered my breath, and I could breathe there, in that desert. Native, Native to what, to the land, to our land, your land, whose land is it? Where is my piece of land? How was it taken from them, from me? How will it be returned to us?

Native to the land…

Allow for the spontaneous healing of body, mind and spirit, as a form of spontaneity in ritual: the allowing, of free flowing energy and ideas to come through. In many cases, people fear participating in ritual, until they are already participants, unknowingly, or are led by another to the experience. Ritual can shake a person from the rigidities of ego that wants to limit experience and growth.

Egos are released through ritual allowing a presence, of being in a new and different life altering way. Likewise, a disease releases the ego, and allows Spirit to enter, allowing and paving the way for deep and profound transformation where soul purpose may be located.

The story cycle of those who walk this path stem from our initiation into this calling; Ritual is an art, an art that weaves and dances with symbols that rejuvenate participants. Everyone comes away from a ritual feeling deeply transformed. This restoration is the healing that ritual is meant to provide. This awareness becomes the honoring of our shadow, the hidden parts of ourselves. Ritual provides the recovery of memory, that which we already know, which may be called soul memory.

The high priestess is the shaman, the medicine women, who reclaims the soul memory of the ancestors, and brings the vision from the heavens down to her community on earth.

Medicine people are truly citizens of two worlds, and must learn to keep their balance in the ordinary, and non-ordinary worlds This is a challenge for many modern day shamans in some respects as there is no formal initiation, the initiation process may come as a surprise, as far as it's lengths and depths, as well as it's true purpose and intention. As in the Native American Spiritual tradition, the elders, matriarchs, mentors, and guides are of great importance, in the Jewish and African traditions as well. The absence of wise support in American society has created a society of fear, isolation, and confusion.

The place for ancestral remembrance and mentors is great. This is true along the healing journey of a physical illness, which requires an integration of the past, present, and future, as well as psyche, soma, and soul.

The medicine wheel of many native people is similar to the ancient medicine wheels, which is symbolic of the five elements that form the cosmos....

In describing community, we reflect on the power in gathering and engaging for rituals of fire, water, earth, mineral, and nature.

We are the land. To the best of my understanding, that is the fundamental idea that permeates Native American life. The land and the peoples are the same, we are of the soil and the soil is of us, the earth is the source and being of the people, and we are equally the being of the earth.

Honored and privileged to have led rituals for women underneath the desert moon, in Austin, Texas, where part of the spontaneously inspired collective ritual enabled each woman to invoke her own prayer, as a vehicle for her own personal, self-designed ceremony, a circle within a circle. This ceremony was a vehicle for inviting and allowing these

The pervasive loneliness and isolation that runs deep as the river in the West, without a supportive community, is equated with the anonymity which results, when culture suppresses true expression of emotions, as in the diagnosis of a person or people with a life threatening illness. This in turn leads people away from what they most deeply want to focus on.

Going back to the soul's purpose, which has enabled and fueled my active pursuit and long standing quest to understand the role of community, ritual, and healing, we turn to the idea of the community safeguarding, and reflecting back the soul purpose of each individual within it and awakening the memory of that purpose by recognizing ones gifts. The communal role is vital in the remembering of personal identity, the purpose chosen for a soul in the world of Spirit, so a person may heal on all levels.

This healing is held by the guru, high priestess, shaman, medicine woman, who uses community ritual, as well as one on one ritual, to channel the holy light that she or he carries and is blessed with upon her hands, her heart, her soul. As her purpose was chosen, she was hand picked, to serve as the vessel, for the Divine Buddha, Great Goddess, Great Spirit to help others awaken, and be liberated from suffering.

The Innocence, the change of a century: of longing for that which has escaped and elapsed with time, journeying into the unknown depths of sexual mystery, mastery of our own bodies, psyches, beings…our unique oneness that has opened up with the creation and de-creation of eternal matters that face all of us today, and have faced our grandmothers, mothers and those ancestors before them. We face the test of bridging the gap of eternal wonders, of the magic that brings us and everything in this world into being, how can we face such a grand mystery often falling short of a concrete answer, a concrete, definition or response to what in the world we are doing here and here to do, how we arrived and how we continue to create our own lives and destinies, filled with misery, of nonsense, or filled with joyous meaning in depth of perception.

Ask yourselves now what is your perception of the world, as it was meant to be, how it was meant to evolve or continue in its creation, the turning spiral of evolution, now ask yourselves how have you become a part in that CO-creation, why are you here, and how are you to serve this world?

If you could create a diary filled with your deepest desires, your unfulfilled longing your sacred passions that have gone unspoken, untold, how would it begin…who would you be writing, speaking to, and in what tone, voice would your dream world look like, your fantasy life look life, ask yourself

Now in sweet silence-

Feel.

Tombs of the Sacred and Profane:

The sacred surge of anima coming through the definition of destruction, changing the reoccurrence of the way we enter and remain faithful to our own truth.

How do we live in radical honesty, in the face of our anger and remain true to the sacred core aspects of the divine within us all

This is the sacred opportunity to transform fear-based energy into sacred love.

Igniting and allowing the power of the Divine Feminine Buddha, goddess, to come forth from within and guide our journey through the darkness, to feel sacred power while being reborn, remade, reformatted and remembered.

Sacred Remembering of who we truly are

Sacred Transformation of who we are to become

Sacred Power of Presence

Love ...BEING... true.

Being true to the struggle. The definition of the word "Israel" is to struggle with Spirit. As I reflect on the meaning of anger in my life, I see that it has been and continues to be a struggle with Spirit, when and how am I trusting that I am held, taken care of, my desires are being met, that all is in perfect Divine order. This in essence is our shared story line, and cycle of survival. There is a survival by smoke and mirrors (pretense), by subsistence, by stonewalling, by sedition, by surrender. I have been peeling back the layers, the masks, seven lives of authenticity. The transformation has either begun or is reaching a plateau of its final stages. In stories of Changing

Woman, and one's plight to "find some reason to continue with

their struggle," even of the edge of the darkest despair."

Here with you.

Within every sad dark corner

There is a miracle waiting to unfold

Unravel, awaken, brought forth, birthed

Into existence, reality, from the deepest

Recesses of the heart. The mind. The soul.

Forgiveness is the great healer.

It walks with you down the road unknown

Inside of the caverns where you must

Create your own light to share.

She kisses you on the forehead and loves what you have taken from her, mother earth, every woman on the planet without permission. Gives back to you, what you were trying to forcefully grab-take- to receive, yes receive, maintain, create internal feelings of power and control of your own destiny, of your own life. It is a mixed bag.

You came into this world with a mission and a destiny and a whole lot of opportunity to make choices along your pathway. You can step on or off of it. Many times we must step off to know we are off, to learn, heal and grow a little bit, or a bunch. When we get bumped off, rocked off hard, and come back to our core center power, we shift into remembering that nothing is worth giving up the freedom joy = peace and love that we worked so hard to awaken within us until we shook a hundred times over to peel off the layers of false wisdom and masks masking what we hoped to overcome and we had achieved

that which we thought we were here to do.

Where god lives.

Where you live. Where you speak from. Where your wisdom

lies if you give it a chance to answer and speak its secret-ness.

Its oneness. Its deep love for all beings.

That is you. You are the one who knows that all beings are you.

Unanimous-synonymous with all that is you – all that you own,

all of your memories your collective conscience is begging you

to hear the sometimes of

Yes, lets take care of each other.

The truth is unfolding reality. Unknown. Once is becomes known you have the choice of holding it.

Pushing it away stuffing it down, to the sides, with a variety of methods. Once you decide to hold it.

Holding the truth without attacking yourself.

Self-compassion. Wins.

Intervention. Intimacy.

Intimacy is the beautiful art of coming into close connection with another, with yourself, with life as it appears before you in the moment-to-moment flow of experience.

Passionate Engagement: An opportunity to share our selves nakedly, being fully honest, vulnerable, take the risk of being seen as we truly are. We dive into the realms of the sacred.

Emotional Sobriety. Powerful place of healing and potential. Strength in the face of rejection. To ensure emotional stability independent of external circumstances.

Developing unshakeable, Emotional ROI – We navigate different levels of intimacy to keep our selves and others feeling emotionally safe.

Investment. Timeless Holdings.

Sublime sensory absorption and alignment with the deep hear to the feminine.

What is your currency-how do you flow in and with life?

The currency you operate inside of your domain, is the modus operandi of the world you create. Is it is the currency of inner wealth, and spiritual capital matrix you work within?

How do we create and operate inside of a matrix that redefines who we are at a core level? Rebuilding authentic lives.

Society. Illusion. Novelty.

Why wear the mask?   Try on your own experience.

Wear the experience.

Of light. I am the light.

Light of Friendship: Shining down on you.

For the night.

For the moment.

Friendship + Love. Could mean a slight touch on the shoulder, or letting someone know you see them. Hear them. Reach out to let them know you see their pain. Could mean a smile, or a kind look.

Love goes a long way.

Get to the heart of who you are.

Business + Ethics = Bringing Sacred Back to Business

Sexy. Kind is sexy. Humble is sexy. Sexy is your inner knowing coming out to play. Showing you can dance – move-play in any game, on any stage, and be one with it.

No agenda. Allow the flow. Connection. Allow another to look into you. Your eyes.

It all starts with investment. Rich. Poor. What are you going to do with your one and precious life? Where are you going to spend your energy, your dollars, your time? Why?

It boils down to the gut-wrenching question we must ask our selves, today.

Emerge. Merge.   With what makes you wake up in the morning. What makes you dream.

Truthful Mergers.

Master the merger.

Master the courage to have the conversation.

Master the courage of conviction.

Live Fierce. Master the conversation.

We come together to hold space for the conversation. For others. Really we come to hold our selves in our own rose warm swabbed blanket of comfort. Comfort we yearn for. We reach for in the night. We ache for in our bellies.

We deflect the conversation. The confrontation. The confrontation with our own uncomfortableness with our inner truth at that moment.

Ask our selves the questions-what is there to fear really?

Interfacing fearless.

Conversation + silence.

Interfacing fearless.

The movement and meditation interfacing

Stillness + breath interfacing

Fearless.

Face = fear interfacing breathless

Wildly pure intentions.

Unyielding + raw =authenticity

Reborn fearless.

Mergers Emerge-fearless.

Resolve: interfacing fearless

Create peace.

Evasion. Erosion. Moment you deflect your truth for the sake of protecting another.

This is the work. Core. Morsel. Detail. Moment.

Tongue of fire: interfacing fearless

Raw heart-peace pulsing

Wildly pure pulsing heart coming to protect

Melt. Raw. Love.

Create. Protect. Destroy.'

Styleless.

Travel in dialogue. To the tips, to the tiers. Travel to the heart of your passion.

Persuade it to stay alive.

Powerful linking

Capacities of the mind +divinity of the heart= transformative power of compassion

Potent formulas of vibration.

Power by nature.

Live fierce.

When you have nothing and are searching you have forgotten who you are

When you have been given everything you have come to remember all has found you

You are everything and nothing, you are the god we are all searching for, the all that we run from.The everything we long for, you are the we that has eluded and unfolded the lining of our very essence. We run to remember that we are no longer lost, we have collected the data and have enfolded the embossed leaf in a jar, we pull it out and remember, the I that is you that is me.

Allowing. For all to be. As it is. Now.

What do you see in the white space? Between the lines? That hide you from yourself.

The trip to Oregon was one to tie up loose ends, in my mind. Close the doors on a possibility of a lost love, a chance to breathe fresh air, after 115 degree staleness of Phoenix summer air, and lastly a way of life. Jalen says your so city like now, your hair is so non-natural and when I asked if I was cuter now, he said no.

Older, hopefully wiser, I waited for the opportunity for Jalen's affection for six years. As it turns out, the young, savvy, and sexy artist, had been sick for the last year. Very sick. To the point where he had to walk with a cane, lost half his body weight and had been on for the last year and a half. He cooked for me, gourmet I must say, although that was the highlight of the tour back to memory lane. We walked to the coffee shop where we first met, and walked past the house I lived in with ten other alternatively life-styled folks. There I slept on the floor in a tiny room, and did massage in the basement to support myself. It was a community of healers, that were involved in risqué free flowing lives, including orgies, polyamorous relationships, naked jacuzzi fun, and supporting each other, while driving each other crazy with drama.

I became the muse of an older creative genius who drove a black jaguar. He woke me up with placing fresh fruit into my mouth, after I went to bed I woke up to him night after night meditating at two a.m. downstairs in the living room, what a sight. It was a world of exploration, art, sexuality, and fresh air to be sure. So many gurus on the path in all shapes and sizes, ages, and forms.

I was in Portland, after a small stint in Ashland, after a Rabbi I knew hooked me up with a housesitting opportunity, one of many I have had. A professor was going to Germany for the summer. That summer I met and studied with many different shamans, received my first set of tarot cards, my first session with a sound shaman that sang to me like a world class opera singer, along with a protector of trees, literally and politically. She said I was a reincarnation of Diana the Huntress, a regular Artemis, I would come to know in the years to come through my doctoral studies.

My best friend of seven years, came to visit me there amongst other beautiful organic locations I took up residence or, was temping at. He came for the Sabbath, he grew up an Orthodox Jew in Queens. Son of holocaust survivors, and a PhD in Psychology, he was honest, loyal, and the greatest friend a person could ever know. Boy did I know him. Well, not in the biblical sense. George, was for all intensive purposes celibate, as I was for those seven years of orthodoxy, four of which were in Israel. He dabbled a bit here and there in sexuality, although I was the "woman" in his life for seven years since I landed in Los Angeles after the break up of my three week pseudo marriage and three month plight of annulment. For in Israel the law of the land states that the female or wife, chattel, is the property of the male, or husband, and does not have right to break of the marriage unless the male party agrees. In my case, my then husband, did not agree. I forfeited all the monies on m property contract, and created a scheme, to release myself from a false and dangerous in many ways, union.

I stayed at my Rabbi's home in the West bank during this time. Alone at the house at times, fearful for my life at times. Drove in unprotected cars, and hitchhiked with fellow Jewish bank dwellers I did not know. I was grateful to my Rabbi and his family who married us, and then had to escort me out of the home I had chosen, with two other men. I remember, having to have my underwear checked by the Rabbis to see if I was bleeding or not, which was an indication whether I was then available be with my husband sexually. I drove in a cab, with enormous diamond earrings, in my ears that hurt and jabbed out redness and pain, of you are my property, and this is how I bought you. It was very surreal. Something out of a horror film, ones I never watch, due to my extreme sensitivity to scary movies. Although this one I had thought I wanted more than life itself. I wanted to be wanted and belong to a family more than air.

I had waited for seven years, and he had waited seven years, and it just seemed like on paper everything fit, although it was an imaginary fit for an imaginary world, that thrived in patriarchy and what strived to be on the side of sacred.

I learned how to be a Jewish woman during my years in Jerusalem, and walked the path, cobblestones, prayed at the temples, danced as Miriam, as she did 3,000 years ago with the timbrels in the holy land, serving the god that was hers and hers alone, at the same time, the worlds, the universes god which was inside of her heart.

I came to know what I did not have, and who I was not. I came to know the depths of intimacy of highest and holist inner nature of the inner workings of the higher realms through my story of esoteric mysticism with many teachers, and many holy books, but most of all, my holy voice came to my in silent meditations on the mountain top in the west bank, where god, my inner heart told me to stay and not go back to the US. It was a voice that I absolutely could not deny as my truth singing to me, whispering to me, and it has taken me fifteen years to unequivocally follow what is my own truth, my own inner voice, my higher self, my inner knowing every and each time.

George, was my rock, and my confidante, my mentor, advisor, my everything, except for sex. I would speak of George while in bed with other men, and realized that my love for George was true, and real. When I drove him to the airport one morning, I realized just how deep that love truly was. I shed some tears, and then sent hi off on his way.

It was a few years later that we took a two year hiatus from our friendship, and then came back for a short while. I had met, studied with and fell in love with a Zen master, guru teacher, with long black hair and crystal clear blue eyes of love one day in Austin, Texas. I had moved there on a whim, or as I would have said, I was guided there, after living in Orange County, well if you could call that living. Homeless on a boat, on a plane, anywhere, I sometimes think I was testing the gods to see if they were with me, protecting me, did THEY have my back? Yes, they did, and boy did they ever. I ended up living in a mansion with a man who expected nothing of me. He was gracious and kind, wealthy, and was supportive. I was a bit overweight then. He wanted what all OC men were looking for, a skinny girl. So I happened to lose a great deal of weight before my move to Austin, and all of a sudden he was all about the new me. Skinny bod and all. I had made up my mind, and had arranged a place, a sweet furnished condo. I was excited to venture out into the world again. Always a new world, a new adventure. One I was ready for. Almost as if I had the chance to start a knew each time I moved. There were many, many moves.

Dallas was part Native American part German. He wore blue jeans and t-shirts, and drove a golden chariot, or a beat up old chevy truck. He was from the stix, Wyoming I think it was, from a family of folks who stuffed animals for a living, he had been through his own ringer, had a son, and became celibate, as I was for seven years, ever since that one interaction. He was a true teacher one that just happened to wake me up in the middle of nights with tantric energies that gave me sexual pleasure I could never explain to anyone. One that taught me how to find true peace within, with Zen meditation, when I was losing it, and had nowhere or what to turn to, I turned within, and found all that I had been searching for.

This was the beginning. I started a formal meditation practice, and saw Dallas twice a week for a year. For three hours each at times. I turned my loft into a palace, temple of worship, with gorgeous silks and scarves, and many candles, which were all lit when he arrived. He was the greatest guest of honor. He walked like candle, and taught me to look inside of one as if I was the light, the teacher the one who stood still and bestowed love and light, divinity, and fed all that stood before me. His gaze was like no other form a different world, one of pure love.

I began to have the sense that I was to take on a guru name. I had my eyes and ears and mind peeled for any messages or clues of what that name would be. I decided to enter a weekend workshop at an ashram, which taught Calligraphy and Zen. As I walked into the prayer hall, I walked around the meditation hall while doing a walking meditation and was struck like lightning at the enormous painting of The Deity Tara, who was green and had a white little dog in her arms that resembled my dog to a tee. I was startled, and when I went up to her statue in the middle of the room I heard the name. There was still some work to be done, and I certainly did not think it was time to take on this name that had just been given to me.

One night I was invited to a party, on a Friday night, I was wearing pink flowing and jeweled dress. I felt anxious, falling into a panic attack that someone was following me, as I had a slight paranoia about such things, since the last few years of being followed by my exes family, and others. I called Dallas. After that I entered the party, everyone asked who I was channeling that night? What deity, what angel? I did not know what they meant, or were meaning by that comment, although I did notice I felt extremely calm, loving and serene. The woman who was hosting the party did not at all seemed pleased that the Native American Shaman, priest like figure was speaking this way to me in front of everyone. On my way out of the event, I was invited to another gathering. For some reason, I felt I was to say yes, and attend. I drove on some dirt pathways to get there, not my favorite, unless I am in a big truck or jeep meant for roads of such nature. I did feel guided to go, so I muddled through. When I arrived, there was a man that fainted in my presence, when I walked int he door. I had seen such a thing happen once before, at a time where a woman said to be an incarnation of a female Buddha deity had been walking and speaking and someone fainted. It was astounding. I was not in a "thinking" space, just a being space as I recall.

This party was in honor of a naming ceremony of a woman who had cancer, and was adding on a name to help change her course of destiny to one of health and healing. It turned out that she was a great devotee of the goddess white Tara, and we had an immediate connection and bond. I had mentioned to her about the intuition I was having and my teacher confirmed that I was at some point to take on a new guru name. I decided I would join her in a fire naming ceremony. Sacred Fire. She gifted me a large Buddha book as remembrance for the night and the bonds we shared. I blessed her with deep healing, and drive home.

Life returned to normality if there ever was such a thing in my life. The days were filled with healing ventures. Men would come from all over. Some were on their deathbed, some were in perfect health. They came from near and far. It was an honor in many cases, especially when they were very sick. The ceremony had its depth, intimacy and gravity, as in some cases it might have been their last.

Some people have asked how I got started healing. Well, I began formally learning healing techniques in Jerusalem. I got certified in Swedish massage, and polarity therapy, Breema, and other bodywork and energetic modalities. I studied reflexology, chakras, Hakomi Body-Centered Psychotherapy, and other therapies once I came back to the states. I remember. I was twenty-three years old when I gave my first massage healing session.

The lady arrived, and when the healing session was over, she forgot her purse and monies and everything when she left. She said she was in an altered state. Others have had the same response. I had many people share they had their first out of body experience, to one man who paid me many hundreds of dollars extra because he could feel his right leg for the first time since a car accident he had had years before. The prayers, singing, crystals, hypnosis, life coaching, and other works blending as well as using breath work, and meditation in my healing sessions.

Then I started giving readings, oh my. Yes, and when it turned out that I was beginning to help people with the readings, I began to feel overjoyed. After the mediumship, when I would speak to the other side, and contact people's relatives that had passed, I was drained of energies which I did not like. I felt truly was being of service and so I did what I could. Over the years I have had many tarot decks mostly all gifted, and then I passed them along, and received new ones. I believe in passing, gifting along, when you are ready to receive the new. Abundance come when you dish it out.

When I think about my relationships with my teachers, I see that they have been my family, in the true sense of the word. They have been my guides of life and love. Often times have supported me in times of life and death trials. The commitment required and devotion of a true devotee is at a very high level. It is a trust and a spiritual friendship like no other.

The Soul's Journey

Personifying the life force or divine creativity, Pele's heart desire is for us to remember the earth is alive. As an ancestral spirit, the goddess of volcanoes, she is known for her passion and vitality, where integrity and innocence merge, to form the vibrant woman. From the deep core of mother earth, Pele, the goddess of fire, brings in the flame as the red-ochre, and pubic V found 40,000 B.C.E. In her book, Pele's Wish, Pele herself is the very essence of the creative impulse of the universe, while reclaiming the land as the menstrual cycle of our planet.

With the flow of her lava, Pele gives us back new land that has been desecrated in teaching us to honor the endless cycles of life-creation and destruction, and the continuation of the life force through all of it.

In her dance of creation, Pele, begins to activate the sacredness of every soul when she dances the sacred. When you dance to honor the Divine within and without, you awaken the spiritual realm of the creative Pele energy. This energy will give you strength and vitality as you rest in her warm embrace, your own inner expression of truth. Truth is the capacity to feel your own inner reverence, in tune with your own authentic feelings and action of justice. This justice with compassion is the dynamic which transforms ritual into ceremony by infusing the respectful reverence of honoring your intuitive feeling of what is right and wrong for you in every situation.

By lifting your own veils, you will be able to rest in an awakened ascended state of consciousness and ultimate bliss and relaxation, connected and rooted in mother soul memories of the ancient.

The vagina caves of Pele were carved in the shape of female body parts, including the vulva and clitoris, and were used as a hospice for the ill and dying.

While holding my grandmother in my arms, the ones she nurtured and raised me with, returning for a moment to the most important gift the sacred listening of the souls silence, her truth, held by boundless unconditional love.

It is when there is someone there to hold you, in their spiritual heart and arms, someone to see your soul, and know who you truly are, the light, a sacred soul being you have always been, the truth teller of many lifetimes.

It is when your heart opens and allows for love to enter and flow through you; the utter magic feeling of Spirit, of devotion, of truth which grows the quest for humility and utter selflessness. In my heart of hearts, knowing we are never alone, and there is always one or many guides angels, people, beings, whether in spirit or in body form, that love us and believe in and of our worth, and destiny.

All is created anew each day, with new choices being made, and patterns broken, love torn skin woven together with lotion, liquid soul love where all is one thread of devotion. Live in your highest being of reality, of oneness.

My burning question unknowingly led me into the halls and classrooms of my doctoral program, which I had dreamed of two years prior. It was a place where my burning flame blazed and came to a startling head in the garden of my inner world manifest. The goddesses, serpents and or dragons I had been drawing on the walls of my Santa Fe, cottage spilled onto the canvas, and then into my writing, and into my daily life. The darkness of the goddess, the dark mother submerged, is our memory. The symbol of resistance of the dark mother, of the ancient grandmother stones embedded in our psyche, felt and expressed in our bodies, will persist, as she does in the present. The root memory of the goddess continues to dwell within our hearts as soul-life, swimming as we allow her to swim within our lives. It is how we wake to her beauty and reality that affects the rest of our day, our memory of then, that is now, and now that is then.

A truth spoken by a survivor of the concentration camps, he says, "I grasped the greatest secret in history that human poetry and human thought have to impart, the salvation of man is through and in love." During the torturous and horrific experiences and suffering were those brief moments of bliss as he describes them, which allowed for the endurance, in an honorable way, by contemplating the image of a beloved, and in this way, achieving fulfillment.

There is a story that speaks of a young married couple who find each other after the war, bones and skin, skeletons, without hair and teeth, hardly recognizable. As the miracle of their survival, of six million Jews that perished, the man says to his beloved wife, "You are as beautiful as the day I met you." This story always makes my heart skip a beat, as the soul of the person is given testimony, and the endurance of love is seen in its highest form. Acknowledge the divine life and breath that is given, and may be taken at any time.

Why then, do we desperately seek a way out, an escape? Why do we seek answers to questions that have been answered in the form of alcohol and drugs, and various other addictions? How do we carry the soul of the Spirit that breathes life into us, and gives to us an opportunity for infinite possibilities? How do we begin to believe that the giving of love is food to the soul: Liquid soul love?

Suffering is life, and finding the meaning in the suffering is a life worth living.

A dear friend and I were having a conversation about self-destructive patterns. The question she posed was why do we have them? I responded with the notion of allowing the dragon into the cave, into the garden in which it makes a home. The "dragon lady" already lives there, inside of the womb, with all of the healing, grace, passion and fire that are both sides of one coin. All the petals on the rose are needed to bleed red, to bleed blue, to be the color that is worthy of the scent it releases; it is the love and life that lives inside of all of us, the place where all of our parts may rest and call home. To love and accept your dragon is to discontinue her stalking and be the bridge to her peacemaking within her own mask. The face that she hides is taken off and placed on the branch of the tree she guards.

Where does our Pele fire come from? How do we connect with the fire in our hearts with our own soul purpose, life purpose, and meaning? For each one of us it is different. What remains universal is the reverence for life that must be reclaimed, remembered, and held. To make the unconscious conscious through full embodiment is a pathway of personal reflection of past and present, uncovering the art and Buddha nature, inward bound.

The space between breaths, between the worlds, is the holy anima that allows us the difference as we remain and maintain wholeness through understanding. One person's truth is theirs, the way he or she believes they experienced their life, never to be taken away from its divine essence.

The innate holiness of a woman, in essence, the idea of woman as sacred. As far as a woman being the vehicle or pathway for men to reach to reach the Divine Feminine, there are many aspects of this as well. For instance, the Mystic Kabbalists went out into the field every Friday night to meet the Shechinah, Divine Feminine, or Sabbath Bride. In essence, they were connecting with their own inner feminine aspect as a result of welcoming the Divine Feminine into their lives, even if but for one evening per week.

In my meditation practice, I noticed I began to bow to my cushion. The very one that offered me the space for self-respect and nobility. The opportunity to give gratitude for the opportunity, and the gratitude for taking the time to re-member my spirit. To acknowledge that the spirit exists even if we cannot see it. We can hear and feel it.

During the summer in the Ashland hills I was joined by a family of deer that made their camp in the family's backyard. They even came so close as up on the wooden deck which I was told was unheard of for a deer to do. Many years later, I noticed how alive, sensual, and comfortable I felt foraging in the back woods of Prescott when I was renting a home in the National Forest there. The huntress was awakened. Every cell of my body yearned to run with the deer so to speak literally, I felt called to be with them, and maybe they with me. Safe.

Gentle. Sweet. Swift. Endearing. Humble. They speak the language of Being. Purity. Gratitude. Praise.

The hills of Oregon brought many gifts among the freedom I felt amongst the old growth trees and forests. The spirited pixie energies, blowing through the wind, the magical vibrations of magic and possibility, of healing, and growth. Genies, teachers, healers, artists, Sikhs, open-sexual tribes of many colors. Two different purple houses I took up residence in, the color of spirituality. I found cuddle parties, and Sikhs and music that for the first time since Israel touched and moved my soul, so much as to follow some music devotionally.

The purity, I found with Shimshai and Snatam Kaur were palpable, and brought me spirited joy. I enjoyed my sense of freedom in Oregon as a whole. Acceptance, and spirit seekers, and of course nature, as you melt into its wings, that embrace you in greenery that you may be lost. Found in. Hot springs to play in, get clean and open your heart into. There was a retreat I went to in the woods where I rode a bike for the first time since childhood. A woman called Meadow believed I could succeed, and the trees smiled down upon me as I slowly pedaled into the forested pathways.

Childhood, purple banana boat bike. Memories of childhood. Nil. To nonexistent. Pictures do jog my memory, as do some other things. My hair short. The playground across the street.

The playground that was Israel. The mountaintop, the caravan I lived in. They thought I was a princess because I wanted my own caravan.

We found out George had the testosterone levels of a 70 year old man, and when he, with the assistance of an acupuncturist started watching football and throwing the remote at the screen. I knew then that we were on the brink of a catastrophe or at the least in new territory together. George decided he loved me and wanted to propose marriage. I was on the coast of California, on the beach looking for my new home. I told him, that I did not feel that way for him, and he decided to never speak to me again. Broke my heart.

I knew it was for the best. It allowed for others to enter our lives. Space.

Closure. Connection. Love is always present, where true love once was.

Soon after I arrived in Los Angeles, and realized playing in Disneyland was not going anywhere, especially with my second ex-fiancee' CEO of independent wealth, his father died, a surgeon, and left him some big dough money and a multimillion dollar properties in Santa Barbara and LA. Ike was the one who left me post engagement altar. He went back to the states and broke off the engagement. He said it was never based in reality, yeah I thought, except for the parties, and my community I had spent four years building, my heart, my world, a false reality only I was privy to. He had been there and done that, been married, had a child, and left her post marriage. I guess that was not reality for him either. Let's say he had issues, great ones.

However, it seemed that I did not have trouble choosing my sexual partners even though I was celibate. We consummated our engagement a year after we had broken up, and I had broken up my own marriage not based in reality, realizing I had fallen into the exact sort of marriage and left as Ike did. He was my only hope. My only escape, I thought he would take me back into his arms and marry me. Well, he did do one of those things, take me back into his loving, on second thought sexually gifted and alighted arms to feed me orgasms of a preposterous nature, it was the best sex I had ever had until that point. Boy if I was addicted to that man before, I was sure as hell going to hell and addicted to him now.

Ten years later, after we had departed each others lives I got back in touch with Ike, a he revealed having remembered the way I tasted and smelled, and that I was still one of his sexual career highlights. In all of my innocence and purity, I shyly accepted his comments, and after some time talking, letting him now exactly the horrors he had transgressed and how I had a nervous breakdown of sorts after he left and how he used me etc, he was furious ... he still wanted to smell and lick me, so I bid him to the ethers of farewell forever.

Living in Beverly Hills, I was a figurehead for an Orthodox preschool that had just made a million dollar coup de tat and ousted the entire staff, and was using me just to play the part of preschool director, I was out of there in a very short period. I started to lose religiosity, and so did my dress code. No more long skirts, and covered blouses to the neckline. Sexy bohemian here, I come back to you, baby. Where have I been hiding? It took eight months back in the states for me to let go of, and wash away seven years of Orthodoxy, a commitment I lived and breathed and swore by every day. Everything from my diet to my dress to my celibacy, and much more.

I was relived to get back to being open-minded Holly Hare, although did not know who that was, or how to get back to that being. I knew she was not far. So, I was called, yes called to the mountains of Colorado, the land of the hippie trust fund baby. Which I was not a member of, although did belong in the upper tiers, in most peoples eyes? I landed into a basement, became best buds with an African American street performer who was my housemate. He was kind, loving, eccentric if there ever was a human that was, he carried a bird on his shoulder for fifteen years, and then one day a dog came along and ate it.

He loved old movies, and apparently I became after a time, an unrequited love. He threw playing cards on rooftops, for a living, and still kept in touch and was always kind.

He had lost his wife and child to another man, and has never healed.

His smile heals others, and so does his cooking. This little Buddhist town was the Mecca for crashing and burning, from old to new. It was Buddhism, meditation, hiking, new agism, spirituality, and organic food, healing and natural beauty.

Back to her roots she awakens her essence

The tunnels of Jerusalem, underground like I

was. On the edges hidden.

Rebellious, covered arms, shoulders, and

sleeves I toured and prayed underneath the

temple of Jerusalem, I was nineteen, my first trip

to the holy land. I was thrilled to be on an all

expense trip, with fifty other American Jews

between the ages of eighteen and twenty-six.

From reform-affiliated we all "won" scholarships

for an all expense paid tour to Israel, touring

traveling, meeting with political leaders, the catch:

it was an ultra-orthodox trip. One where I would

jump the fence to Mecca, and sneak into the

church of the holy sepulcher said to be a

defilement of the laws of god if I entered their

gates.

I went anyway, of course. I was racing for truth

and adventure. I went alone. It was my little

secret. I went hiking for the first time, and tread

on the footsteps of prophets before me, maybe I had been one of them in a former life, who knew. All I knew was that there was a fall back, a way of life that was a way, of family, strength, direction, structure, and rules, boundaries that were absent in my life.

As I had no rules to speak of imposed upon my life. I imposed OCD rules like matching my underwear to my clothes in high school but that was all I had known. I was so far removed from attention, I had been stashing my mother's clothes in a bag and would change at school at grade three.

I started bleeding at age 10. Had size C breasts at age 13. I would rather attribute it to wearing women's clothes since age 5, then the actual casualties.

All I had known was chaos, screaming,

punishment, terror, and payment for grades.

Wrapped inside our bodies, we take on what is

said to be ours.

Our pain, our wounds, our trappings.

I ran down to the Ultra-Orthodox tunnels, saved

for married women, and soon to be a married

women myself, as in the night before my wedding

night, about to be a married women of the Ortho

cloth. We had made our own choice, taken our

own vows to remain true to the laws, written by

men, to keep women "pure" or holy before the

duty was done. The duty of the man to pleasure

the women, and of course the duty of a woman to

obey her husband. It was a ritual immersion, a

dipping of the highest order, and I bought into all

of this. I believed in everything I was doing in one

form or another with all of my pseudo I think this

is right heart. I was born a Jew and therefor God asks this of me, my blind faith that is, and every law that went with it.

We were accompanied by a woman who helped us prepare ourselves, nakedly dipping three times, making sure all was immersed as we said a prayer to god to help us conceive and help us be servant like, or so I thought. Who knows it was all in Hebrew the language of the gods.

Whose god was it anyway? Mine? A male god? A female god? Was it both? Split into two parts?

The men tried to keep the women tied to their doorpost and their bedroom night post when not anywhere in sight near bleeding time. God forbid. Everything was thank god this and thank god that every other word out of every person's mouth was thank god.

Talk about gratitude, this gratitude was a foaming at the mouth sensationalism of the true times when gratitude was to be felt or spoken, when we spoke an after the bathroom prayer or prayer before a meal, yes this was a forced plea for god to hear our words, our gratitude, but how grateful was each person that spoke these prayers by rote, or was I the only one who forced and faked it till I made it.

There were weekly, daily rituals, gatherings, events, food, ceremonies, 400 weddings I attended in four years, it was one massive celebration of food, god, and festivity, and light, and then there was the mass hysteria to do so, the dark side always came to light without balance.

Over the years, I dated actors from LA in Jerusalem to find god, Beverly Hills trust fund babies who were writing undercover stories for their books or magazines, running away from themselves, families, a life that they hated, traded in for a life that was holy, and good.

Eventually I traded the bus rides in fear of being blown up for cab rides and thousands upon thousands of dollars in an endeavor to stay alive, and not blown to smithereens. It was a holy mind fuck if there ever was one. Right before I returned to the states, during and after my divorcee' status was final, I lived in a building that was "unsealable" from nuclear bombs and missiles with an impending attack from Iran, which really put the seal on my deal to go back to the country I was born and raised in.

While all of my actions, well almost all, spoke to a time where I would become a permanent fixture in the state of the Jews, I knew deep in my heart that I was to excavate and mine my soul, the gold that lay at the center of it all, my heart space, and was to learn and relearn lessons and re - imprint my soul, break and re sculpt my heart. I was meant to return again as I did to tradition, to what I saw was a way to family, harmony, and accord in my early days of passion and adventure.

I called upon that knowledge and that way of life, well I ran back to it almost two years later when tragedy shook my soul, the last year of college.

It was like take a spiritual prescription dosage of the highest quantity with pure and blind faith believing that prescribing and fulfilling my mission through the Orthodox brand and world would heal everything.

Conflict is creative energy wound up so tight, it has no room to breathe. Trapped. Our roots have no room to grow. We have no room to grow. SO we fight. For everything. For space, For Voice. For the chance to be seen, to be heard, to be acknowledged, recognized and appreciated. We fight to win. Win the award, the girl, the boy, the prize, the money, the fame.

I was in the grips and throws of the mining for gold, which is what Dallas called what I have always been searching for. What I asked is that? I asked. He said, " You were mining for gold, its called enlightenment."

Oh, is that what I was doing, I said, never thought of it that way before.

I was thinking more on survival terms, finding love, ravishing morsels of truth, wisdom, adventure.

"Nope it was more the enlightenment bit," he said.

Oh. I said, and slumped down into my armchair. He then told me I drank my bottle of Evian water as if it was alcohol. Oh, I said again, well I'm just grateful I do not drink alcohol.

I worked with this "Returned" Rabbi who had to the fold, a baal tshuva or master of returning Rabbi, to the faith, cloth that is, after being a hippie in Berkeley they say. He had the tiniest office the size of a closet broomstick. You could walk in there and sit down and that was it. All quarters very minuscule compared to the US or anywhere else. When the space was large, you knew some serious cash was involved. Serious millions. Of course, I was like a moth to a flame to those with power, wealth, fame, money, without really knowing it. My sexual power, not yet prowess at the time, pulled in, reeled them in, all of them, jumping on a pogo stick for the lollipop. I was adorned, covered, yet gleamed and sparkled like the jewel I was.

Siren. What was that? The Rabbi, Stanford, said that even if I wore I garbage bag everyone would still be staring at me. Well, I though pouting back to him. I'll show them. At this point sweet Stanford had me to the point in my Orthodoxy which I swore I would never near, at the height of Chassidism, the Meah Shearim type. Who would have guessed the Euro Fashion Model, on club stages at seventeen would not even glance at a man, young or old, short or tall, and would be covered from head to toe literally looking sixteen years old, or so I felt and thought.

I walked on foot so much during my time in Jerusalem, often times I felt like a mule, hauling my groceries home. Panting, and sweating, due to the extreme heat of the desert.

Boy, did I meet the creme of the crop while dating celibately in the holy of holiest city in the world. The melting pot of all that melts. It was matchmaker heaven. After having been to several of them. I was sure that my match would be made. After all, why wouldn't it be. I had everything to offer, didn't I? One woman at the wailing wall said, " Oh, you have made your list of things you would like, but what do you have to offer," I thought she must be kidding, I was 23 years old, and a knockout. My ego had some major repair work to be done over the years.

The visits to the holiest sites, certainly for religious or pious Jews were memorable and visited often. Sites like Hebron were Abraham and Sarah were buried, Masada, The Dead Sea, Rachel's tomb, the hundreds of descents to the wailing wall for unending tears and prayers for every and any occasion, but most importantly my never ending prayer for what I then called my soul mate. Where in the world was he, and why was he not answering my call for him to show up in my life, I always wanted and thought he was coming NOW, like the next moment or the next day. Of course, on my clock, my timing, what I needed and wanted immediately, and why in the world was god not delivering him, I thought over and over again.

The thought of being a lesbian never occurred to me until a man I knew on my favorite mountain top in Israel, one my ex-husband sent to follow me in the Colorado hippie Mecca. I later found

out about this situation, and said to myself, why

don't you just say you found out you were a

lesbian so your ex-husband, would leave you

alone, and not remain suspicious why I suddenly

up and left the family. They were thinking maybe

it was because he himself revealed to be Jewish

Maffia on the honeymoon, threw lamps at my

head, he certainly knew sex was not the issue. I

had saved my re-virginization crowned with a full

blown orgiastic scream and real true orgasm from

standard women on top of man, mind blowing

orgasm at 25 years old. The first one I can recall

consciously, at any rate.

After all of my sexual, "Left the body

occurrences," it went a little something like this,

hey, I'll be gone for a minute while you have sex

with my body, I'll be right back, just let me know

when your done, it was much the same scenario

before the whole celibacy orthodox period started, no pun intended.

I started to explore my own body, had my first masturbation session, along with side dishes of dreams of terror from all of those bus rides in the bullet proof buses in the West bank. It was all a blur in waking hours. I could not believe the culture shock I was experiencing. A fish out of water. That much was clear as day.

Part Three

Sacred Soul, Sacred Body

I met Sam in Sedona, and he is 54 years old and has not been in a relationship for 20 years. He attributes this to his life changing first orgasming at age 13. "'It was life changing," he said, I could not wait for every opportunity to experience this delight.

What he found was the golden treasure, within himself. The ability to experience pleasure and divinity within was touched at a very early age. In a society where this liberation, expansion, and true inner light, and in essence and most importantly life force was deemed the opposite of what it was. As a result, Sam in his later years became celibate and practiced the lifestyle, or spiritual path of self-sex, which he feels is the essence of it all. "Food, Sex, and Creativity." Who needs all the hassles that come with being in a relationship when you can self pleasure yourself, and have an even better experience going at it solo he says.

This is where I come in a dream he had the night before he met me.

He is standing outside a room where the lifestyle is tantra and polyamorous or multiple lover oriented. He feels he does not fit in, or belong, but would like to be welcomed on the next leg of his spiritual journey. He tells me there is a woman that looks very much like me who takes him by the hand and takes him in the room where everyone is, and is he able to experience being with women and multiple partners.

The tantric guru…the spiritual guide ushering men and women into sacred sexuality…he tells me about full body orgasm and how he has been practicing for years, and can now "go for four or five hours." Although I tell him it may be different when he is with woman, and I assure him that he is about to experience a far higher level of pleasure when he is with a woman. He is now ready…

He asks me how this is possible to fuse the spiritual and the sexual…
The key to orgasm is being in your body of light and from there emerging as the light body that you are…all you are is a light body of love…

This light body comes to us through the spirit realm of the oceanic explosion of life giving pleasure…

In the present moment all is real is the breath you follow, when the mind leads you, you are controlling with the ego, in bowing to the breath your divinity blows in and out of you reaching another's voice and breath. As woman we move in our center while surrendering to responding to each movement that is presented in the dance of sacred union…we allow the oceanic flow to bring us to the energetic explosion that is waiting deep within our core to erupt slowly and fully…all of cells will feel blissful when we allow ourselves to be in the flow of the dance…

We are all one

A Jewish family of old

Ancients songs weave through long valley cobble stones roads

That are alleys that hold all of our faces and tears and hearts yearning

Thirsting for that feeling what is that feeling? From where does it come?

I am a weaver of hearts, a weaver of old stories-

bringing people together

by their commonalities, by their love of each

beautiful thread they see in another being.

Another's light that beams into their hearts as

they speak as they share themselves....What

else is there?

Where can we go to feel the love the connection

the power that brings us coming back together

each and every time? Why do we come? So I am

questioning now, now is my time to question.

I was never allowed to question and not know, I

always had to have the right answer to every

question in the face of ridicule and laughter.

Where is your broken nose your slapped face you

shamed eyes that have seen so very much. You

have experienced more than most in many

lifetimes

You are old and you see well, the wisdom seeps

from your eyelids in the form of tears my young

lady friend that is the crone.

You are the web weaver of many and has come

to this world in compassion, women, whose

spirituality was so intense, so deep, so

unconscious, that they were themselves unaware

of the richness, they held.

To suffer, to be, to give to hold.

Weave our own web

Our stories are the Torah of long ago

They are ours

We must find of way of weaving them together

To tell each other stories-our own stories that are

theirs

We must tell their stories

We must not forget

We must remember our stories their stories that

are our

Those women who lived-women who died

Women who laughed women who cried

A beauty queen, model of nothing and everything.

At thirteen years old, I entered a pageant, one for

beauty, and poise, a 2 minute speech, a swimsuit,

and a sexy off the shoulder evening gown. I won.

Remember I looked about 20 years old.

At 21, my entire life changed. I changed it.

Graduated half a year early as I did with high

school. To get out. Just get me out of here, I

thought.

I took the crowd of a few thousand, but who really

knows how many people were in those stands,

bleachers, they were all a blur, to me standing in

a black sheer dress wrap about to give a speech

that started with: I 'd like to take you back in time

for a moment, to a small town in the Ukraine,

called Balta, on the Black Sea. I was the Vice-

president of the class, my fancy title for the fact

that I wanted to get up in front of thousands of

people and tell my grandmother's story of

survival.

I compared my life entering college at nineteen,

although I was really seventeen, now, come to

think of it, and what my grandmother was going

through, her hometown turned into a trapped ghetto. She was trapped, even in her own home while getting married to my searingly handsome grandfather, who later became a war hero, honored for his bravery, and by me at his funeral. There were Romanian guards outside the door, already standing watch, guarding the prisoners they held captive. They fought for food, water, they came our alive, after the war, were still Jewish, no longer religious.

My grandfather was an orphaned at age thirteen and had 5 sisters who were all killed during the war. My grandmother dreamed of becoming a doctor, although due to her marrying she became the embodiment of her surname, an accountant, and a seamstress. They grew their own clothes and potatoes, she and the girls, my mother, and her sister later became seamstresses and moved to the big city were they later met their husbands.

As they were denied access to universities due to their Jewish heritage. What a shame. There I was proud in spite of all their denials. I was honoring them, as they were denied an opportunity to be educated and honored as I was.

It was a moment in time. A snippet. A blippet.

The man that haunted my dreams took them to sit behind everyone, where they could not see or hear me give the speech. After I had provided front row seating for them. It was indeed a shame. His shame. He and a few others would carry to their grave.

They had another chance to see me, hear me, prance along a stage. It was not over till it was over. I had invited the whole family again to be present for my win in another pageant Miss Utah USA. The Russian Jewish clan flew to Utah to stand witness as I wore a white beaded evening gown, and paraded around as if I was going to get first place. Well, I didn't, and far from it. I didn't even place. I blame it on my anti-Semitic notions that when I answered the question about which career field I wanted to go into, and said International Jewish Communal Service work. True or not true, the fact was I did not place, and was humiliated as now they were in the very front row. There it was, the shame that I had carried around me from age four. Open on display for all to feast their eyes upon. Even my boyfriend, a replica of Johnny Depp was to my embarrassment present, to my loss and humiliation.

This was not the catalyst that turned my life upside down. I did hit bottom after that. It was all a blur.

I started writing. Poetry. For many years it only came out as poetry in lyrical prose that I could understand, kept hidden, a secret, a balm for my murdered soul. A way for her to come out from the shadows she lived and lurked inside of.

She went into hiding much like Anne Frank did. Into bunker where no one could or would find or look for her. There were signs to her existence. She would come out in different bedroom scenarios from time to time or when I was scared. She would talk in third person. Constantly asking herself who she was? If she was real? Who was really real?

She was the bad one. They did not believe her. So she must be the one to blame. So it was.

The monstress born of deceptive lies she told herself. About herself. Oh, and then by those who "loved" her most too.

So she internalized and believed herself. Myself. The little girl that was later found.

My biological father, who questioned this fact at some point in my twenties, crushed me time and time again. My nemesis, his wife was an ally in releasing him from my life. He said he was glad he did not fly in to the graduation ceremony to hear me speak.after he had read my speech, I had sent it to him post facto.

Greg, my sperm donor of a father, said it was an embarrassment to the family. I was not sure how that was possible, as I received a standing ovation from thousands of people. He was obviously not one of them. He would step out of my life again, as he did at age 4, and allowed his first cousin to torture my body, and kill my soul.

That is whenI left my body for the heavens for the first time.

He wrote my mother and I a letter when I was around twelve years old. I remember reading it on my bedspread in the house painted black, how strange, and then apropos I thought years later. "You," he said, to my mother, "are responsible for the death of my unborn child, for the stress you have caused me and my wife for child support inquiries. '

I started to bawl; the war had started up again. It wasn't enough that while I was in the crib at age zero, my mother cheated on my father while he was at work, with his first cousin who later married my mother. The war that ensued between a family that was newly immigrated and had no footing on American soil, was in chaos and strife from the moment they landed onto free soil.

My mother felt trapped and wanted to escape the dredges of motherhood and mostly poverty, she was twenty-five the same age I was when in Jerusalem getting married and then returning, she was getting married in Russia, then coming to America. It all circles around. My parents were not invited to my wedding.

In some ways we are all re-enacting our family wounds and patterns to heal them. My mother's brother, whom I did not know ever existed as she never spoke of him, came up one day as she started hysterically sobbing at his mere mention. My mother was never on firm footing in her life, and as her time continued with her newly married perverse, twisted husband who degraded and affected her purity and sense of self worth; she eroded and rode the rage of her own and his fury combined in intimate daily and nightly terrors.

Before I stopped riding buses, I rode many. More than I had ever rode in the states, I was without car, for four years, and upon those bus rides I recited a luminous amount of psalms. Psalm upon psalm upon psalm. I waited to see saints, I walked the streets of tiny hidden streets meant for only those who do not touch, or guard their touch before marriage. I was one of those. Shomeret negia, I guarded my touch for so long, and so carefully that when the opportunity arose to touch a little bit in certain moments, well, if I was dating, engaged, or behind closed doors I would dabble a bit, nowhere near any sex mind

you. It was way off the table. WAY off the table.

There was not even a table to speak of, maybe a

bed. I must have recited more psalms than a nun

that devotes herself to god does in a lifetime, it

was day in and day out. I was committed,

devoted, to my god, the one they said I knew. I

only knew the one I knew, intimately, who was

always there for me. The one that mothered and

fathered me as I was orphaned. Abandoned,

abused, and neglected, he and or she was there

watching, guarding, protecting, I did believe that

the worst had already befallen me, and it was

over, I had to heal. Yes, the worse of it was over.

So what else, what else was there? I placed

myself at risk, risk above all risks. Dozens of

times. In dozens of countries all over the world.

I was devoted to devotion, enthralled with finding that devotion in any and every form, all the holy ways I could serve god.

When I first entered the womb of the sweat lodge I was unprepared for what I would experience. I flopped out of it as a wet baby being born through the tremors and trauma of a birth canal, out of breath, and relieved to be born again.

I crawled on my hands and knees into the small womb like entrance after waiting in a line, or half moon circle to be smudged or feathered off by a smoke cloud of a sage brush, brushing off the auric layers of grime and dirt that had gathered upon my clear flesh and angelic bodice of energy matter.

Dallas once told me it was not the sage itself that did the clearing and cleansing of a space or auric field, it was the actual intention you put behind the prayer, this I knew although it seemed as if I was hearing it with fresh ears, a beginner's mind as he would say in Zen speak.

It was dark with a small hole in the ground or fire pit to the right, women were to the left, men to the right, I think, It was a mixed use, men and women womb facility for sweating out your prayers and getting close to god, the you that was god, all clean and pure.

A vehicle of remembrance. I was dressed in a long gown, the men were not. It was at least 120 degrees in the tepee, with hot coals and Native chants bringing me into a place only prayer and god could enter. A place I did not know, and yet knew very well.

You could not leave, or lay down. You had to find a way to make it through. This journey was a few more steps into hell and then into heaven and back again. What were those again? Did they tell us about that in Hebrew school?

I didn't understand anything there anyway. Ended up becoming some Ortho girl dressed in long sleeves.

It was a miracle I survived the sweat lodge in all of its sacred madness. It was as authentic as it got. It was in someone's backyard in Colorado, I think. Then I went to Sundance in Oregon.

We walked in, after driving a few hours, I forget who even invited us, must have been the gods invitation, we were welcomed, me and my 6 foot five blonde haired blue eyed Sikhish born again Christian rap artist of a lover, who was a vegetarian. Upon entering we were immediately offered buffalo stew to which he declined, and she was offended. We were off to a great start. I knew we had been invited by someone and obviously there for some reason. My sound shaman Joy had mentioned I was going to marry a very tall Native American man so I was hoping maybe he would be around. No such luck.

Especially with my born again friend, whose virginity I unknowingly received or took however, you would like to think of it. I met him at a restaurants bar while we were both eating lunch, and he though his father and I might get along. His father was a 65 year old Sikh. He began writing me love letters. However, his son came over to my home, and I wrote love letters unknowingly to all parts of his body. Including his virgin parts, which he told me about after the fact.

I was imploding and exploding about how could I have done this. Well it was done. Enough said.

So, there we were, in the middle of the sacred wounding stabbing ceremony the men go through where they dance for great spirit, and mutilate their bodies in reverence and deference for what great spirit would like them to sacrifice for. It now seems so Christian like I suppose.

I only have come to know Jesus in the past two years. HE has come to me in a few visions, and has been with me in spirited weekly prayers, weekly through my final lifetime beloved spiritual father, mentor, and teacher Ashoto.

There were other lodges, one led by a Mayan man, and a few Native friends on Mt. Shasta, and another in an all women, all naked sort of celebration in another backyard. The final one being that of Ms. bluebird herself, in a small lodge she had built for women in Sedona.

She showed us how to make tampons for the days when the apocalypse would be upon us and we could not go to the store and buy it. I was surrounded by people who knew much more than I did. Until all the pieces and bits of information started falling into place.

I was shown how to magnetize all that I wanted, to myself, and how to release all I did not need. I was taught to protect the energies around me, call and move, merge, and cultivate them, I was the shaman I was always was. The calling was energetic medicine one seer told me during one of her lectures at the Mayo Clinic. Energy

Medicine what was that really, I thought to myself.

I knew I was intuitive, and she was a medical

intuitive, maybe thats what I was? What was I

exactly?

I had been in touch with so many intuitive people,

ones that had access to information beyond the

beyond, into the spirit world and beyond. Other

forms of life, and death were summoned and

sought after, I was one who trusted and believed.

At times, I had become dependent on these

psychic advisors, who became close friends,

none of them became sexual, there was one that

was very tantric in nature, but that was all. Well,

the true love sometimes morphed into other

feelings and thoughts that were never acted

upon, but desired.

Healers and psychics were my best friends, my confidantes my worlds, my own personal connection to the world, and my inner circle of spiritual family. The bonds were strong and almost unbreakable, until they were, always devastating, like the loss or death of a mother, father or husband.

Gino was an Italian healer who came from a long line of witches in Sicily. He had magic powers, and I met him in a bar one night with a group of his friends, in a small town in Charlotte, North Carolina. He pulled snakes out of my back, an exorcism, who knows, but it sure felt like one. It was like nothing I had ever experienced, and I had never seen poltergeist. I was too terrified after I saw Friday the Thirteenth and Nightmare on Elm Street at age thirteen to ever watch a horror movie again. I had my own I had to watch at night, thank you very much.

I was house sitting again, yes in the woods, for a friend of a friend, a lesbian who thought I was her soul mate, and so we became good friends, she lived in Charlotte, and arranged for a summer tour de France for me there, while her lesbian friend went out of town. I was taking care of the cats in a mountain cabin in the middle of nowhere, well I guess somewhere since I could drive half an hour to Charlotte.

One morning I woke up, with a message from the angels, and my guidance that said its time for you to get a dog. A dog, I had never had one before, but this was the time. Here goes nothing and everything. The voice would not stop pestering me and I had to listen. So I tried and fought for a little pug I though was cute, the gods were not having it. I ended up meeting my destined fur child in a parking lot, she was white, small, and dressed in a pink tutu. No way, I said as I took one look at her feminine form, and pathetically crying eyes, rescue me, take me, SAVE me.

I did decide to hold her, and from that moment forward I knew she was mine.

She has taught me how to love, and be loved, how to respect and honor, nurture, and care for another living being. I remember my biological father once calling me on the phone, he said you do not know love until you have a dog. I did not have any idea what he was referring to, until I had my own.

One day, Greg, my biological father, drove a few hours to visit me in Monterey Bay as I was in the area with a client, at the Eden Retreat Center on the coast of California, attending a healing weekend workshop. As we walked along the docks edge at a nearby lake, he began to tell me this story: Tatiana, and Greg were at a dog fair, and someone came up to him before they entered the fair and placed a Rhodesian Ridgeback in his arms, he said that from that moment on, he knew that the dog was his." He gave the dog back, and ended up with Prince, the German Shepard, he grew to love but was not "his." Upon his wife's insistence Prince was held in the garage at all times, until one day when they left him in the back yard and went away for a few days on vacation. Prince, jumped the fence, and dashed out of their lives.

He told me of his broken heart, and I knew he had a history with heart attacks in the past, so I later assumed he meant to tell me that was the story, my story, the story he had with me.

He was afraid to give 'money" support to my mother as he did not believe they would use it to support me, and use it for themselves. It was a battle he opted out of, and as a result, opted out of my life.

Unconditional love comes from the heart of heaven, the one that lives in your own chest, to open and awaken to this is indeed the awakening the great orgasmic awakening we yearn for with all of our might.

The race for fame and glory, riches and beauty, does not compare to the feeling of giving and receiving true love, of belonging of sharing, and caring.

Sacred Commitment.

I committed to be of service. I committed to being a healer.

I committed to doing anything and everything it took to heal.

The journey was SACRED.

I journeyed into the sacred realms of reality and illusion.

I took many there and back as well.

Shale was a successful engineer I met at the Colorado National Park, one day while I was debating which path I was going to walk down, become a crazy female feminist interfaith Rabbi, do a Phd in spiritual studies, or travel the world again.

The first two were really in the running. I heard him playing guitar as I was walking and sat by his side and listened. It was beautiful and true. It turned out that his wife of twenty years whom he had built a custom house for in Aspen, reduced his playing to the basement only. I started seeing visions, and felt into the depths of his music. It was a healing music of sorrow from the crevice of the soul that had shame interlaced with fear and love running throughout its chained memories. He was letting his soul out to play in the sunlight, and honored me with a listen. I became friends with Shale and he later became a healing client. I taught him about energy and clearing his home, helped him write poetry and paint his emotions, and when we spoke he shared he was, a childhood survivor of sexual abuse at age thirteen.

He helped an orphanage for girls, I was volunteering at. While I did not have much myself, I was sharing some poetry workshops with the girls.

He donated a recording studio to the center.

I did not really have any possessions and decided to go off to a ten day retreat of silence in the back woods. It was ten of the most challenging and rewarding of my life.

I lost ten pounds, ate vegetarian organic, woke at 4 am everyday to meditate, my body broke, and ached with each sitting, I fell in love with a woman there. Watching, Gazing, as most people did with me, we fell in love in silence with what was before us. This woman was very tall, long blond, hair about twenty-five, arrived in a white Volvo wagon which she said was her forty year old boyfriends whom she lived with. She was true, ate salad like she had three stomachs, and had a space altar of a few sacred things above her bed. Wooden bunk beds, in a shack. All of our writing utensils, and electronics were back in our own respective wagons, mine happened to be a black Volvo, don't ask me how I chose it, it was the energy of the era of coming back from the holy land, I did not know what was up or down in the buying of cars. I did know what I liked, what could have been mine, like the Rhodesian ridgeback but chose something else entirely, something that was not mine, and something I returned to the lot after the ten days were over. I had made it, watched little ants intently and dreamed of a little white BMW, and then with all of my might I believed, and Shale bought me a new car. The only one to ever do so. Not a spouse or a boyfriend.

I did walk in on him masturbating, it was a surreal scene. The fan was blowing as he was in his bedroom, I tried to knock but he did not answer, focusing on his intentions, his eyes closed a huge white sheet and his hand jacking off, I was praying he was not thinking of me but I knew he was.

Reminds me of the time I was on a train in Moscow, heading towards St. Petersburg to visit some friends and there was a man masturbating to the sight and or sound of my body. It was an overnight train, and yes, I was stunningly, that is stunningly stupid, and insanely traveling alone.

I almost vomited, held my breath, and exited the train, it all seems like a long lost dream. I exited the train car, and was met by my Russian friend whom I had met in America. I was his guest. I fell in love with his best friend, they both saw me off at the train station with a rose in hand, in love and around betrayals, I fell in and out of love so many times.

It was all true. Most of it was not a dream.

He was going to meet me on the other side. He supported my spiritual endeavors, and fell in love with me at the same time. I did not return the feelings.

It was a difficult break, he said he was not ready and did not want to heal. I could not understand how he was not ready to heal after so many years.
I was sure he was not thinking of his ex-soul murdering wife while doing the wild thing with his leg.

He sent me spiritual contraptions in the mail before our California trip, while I was in Ashland, Authentic Tibetan bowls, chakra stones, a golden goblet which signified reincarnation of a deity I later found out about, all of which was the real deal and must have cost a fortune. Well, I was his spiritual mentor...

It all came to a screeching halt in California when after nights on end of playing music and his drinking Mike' Lemonade by the beach.

I was still not romantically involved with him, after he had given me everything I said I had wanted in his mind, and in my mind I was strictly his healer, helping him to heal.

We were done, and another lesson learned, another chapter closed. He was dating a lovely woman whom I hope he is now very happy with.

There was a client that came in with cancer all over his body, in patches, black, red, as if he was about to pass any moment, and he knew it, and told me so, he was also about 400 pounds, and could hardly make it up the stairs. It was difficult not to vomit at first. It was even more challenging to touch the actual skin let alone speak or do anything else. It was only when I opened the session with a candlelit ceremony and a calling in of his angels and guides was the sacredness of the moment revealed to me, and the strength to carry on, was as easy as eating a morsel of chocolate.

His last wish, his deathbed, he was nurtured and cared for, and it was sacred pleasure and closure. Blessed, anointed and nourished as most of my clients came to me for. Most were surprised by the purity I blessed them with. Many mentioned

the generosity with which I touched them with.

There was a teacher in Oregon, who had a castle

I took up temporary residence in for a few weeks,

I think. She had me clean her floors with a

toothbrush. It was one of the crazy gurus you

hear about that make you wash their floors for

Zen like practice, she said I needed to learn how

to chop water, and carry bricks, I mean carry

water, and chop wood, yes thats it.

Well, I finally did get down on my hands and

knees and prayed I was would find my hot diggity

gold, pack my bags enlightened as she was, and

call it a day. Nope, no such luck. I was struck with

a dream that night that the stern faced, lovingly all

knowing channel of information that streamed out

of her mouth was an enormous white spider, that

appeared in a the form of a creature that scared

the living daylights out of me, and I awoke

packing my bags instead of being lit on fire of the

spiritual kind, I was running for the hills. The flat

kind.

She told me not to be afraid of her. She said she

was unique, very rare, I think she may have said I

come from the same place she did. Now, I may

agree with her to some extent. At the time, I was

appalled. She was full of rigidity and wisdom from

the stars, I could not make sense of it, even for all

of my journeying and such, it was dished out in a

way that I could just not swallow raw.

Raw. Kind. Organically made =love.

As it is.

 I did not even know what the hell tantra was, let

alone any idea of the fact that I was going to

learn, teach or knew its essence in the deepest vibrational core of my spirits essence.

It was the furthest thing from my mind, until I started having visions of a tantric temple in class. Then I had more visions when visioning my future life. It was coming to me from source energy.

To make love organically, spiritually, from inside of yourself.

Yes, I guess I definitely asked for it. Since love was what I thought I was in quest for. All of this shamanic walkabout stuff, where was my love already handed to me on a silver platter? I was a demanding raw, bitch at times, many would attest to, and then there were times along my path of healing that I evolved into beings of pure love and oneness that were otherworldly.

The integration of the two worlds.

I could never have imagined, or dreamed up the life I led. Seven years celibate. Seven years the sensuality queen of tantric mastery. I was a breech baby and always joke that I do everything backwards, as I was scheduled to come out that way, and felt unwanted, wanted to climb back in to the hole, the womb tomb, from the stars of heavens gate.

I dreamt I was falling into a dark hole filled with light upwards, looked like the universe filled with particles, falling upwards, I was terrified and eerily not falling in fear. When seas collide, and you know. You have met your love mate. The one destined and chosen for your mission in this lifetime. All worlds fall to the way side to make room for your momentous re-union. It is like no other feeling in this earthly world.

You are no longer ships passing in the night, you pray that with one glance, he re-members you. Everything, about you hint and whisper, y everything you will say or have done is accepted, however much has been traversed by both lives for you to come together. How much strength, conviction, and dedication to what is true. For both of you to be on your paths at the same time when meeting. You begin to see all the patterns that led you forward and back on the blades of and in insanity and love.

Truth you will never lose. Falsity fades away. On and under duress your heart breaks open for the one you love, the devotion you feel, as he passes you in the hallway. I thoughtI was going to fall over, and re-member feeling ecstatic that day, I could not stop smiling, and put on a lace bra

underneath my dress. It was a strange feeling. I

went to an Indian restaurant for lunch, and

ordered the Tandoori chicken, which was brought

out in style, fit for a queen I say, out loud. It must

be a special day, and believed it.

The hot young, waiter looking in my direction

could not keep his eyes off me which already

made my day as I checked out his biceps with

scorpion tattoos on them. I asked him what they

signified, silly me, his astrological sign, he said in

broken English. I smiled right out the door,

preparing me for what made me all hot and

bothered in my Mercedes, which is the reason I

had to pull over first. I just was feeling hot and

bothered and could not for the life of me figure

out why.

I had always been a huntress, the sexy steamy

kind, of course, but liked to get raw and dirty out

in the woods as well. I always used to say,

a five star resort was my way of camping.

However, a very large part of my wildness did

come from being in and around natural

surroundings, I just did not love to sleep on the

floor, although made it my home quite often for

someone who preferred sleeping on six count

threads.

I chose the men. I saw them, picked them up, and

seduced the ones I wanted. Looking back at how

women throw themselves at men these days, it

truly is a reverse squabble of a messy situation.

One that has the wheels of the birds and the bees

puzzle screwed on backwards indeed. I foam at

mouth thinking about how it was that I pointed the

bow and arrow into cupids heart, and for some

reason they decided to only stay the night, if even

that long. George used to call me the temp girl, and asked me and then I asked myself when was I going to get a full-time job, and become a wife? My mother was asking herself the same question for about 15 years. She thought she just had to get me through phd school. Boy was she ever mistaken.

We broke up, my mom and I, that is, after 35 years of serious trouble, and many pseudo divorces prior, after having fallen slave and slain to her warrior like battle cries and pleas, suicide threats, and droppings on the floor feigning seizures etc, to get her way, getting me to fall on the floor myself during the first job I ever received. She was so proud, a youth director of a fancy Jewish Community center in southern Connecticut. She took me shopping and bought me all new clothes. I had just spent the summer losing about 35 pounds after gaining it the year before while in Jerusalem.

One of my stints, the second out of five trips to Israel, ended with my staying with an Orthodox couple who were into sexual web cams, and offered my participation as a favor or? Not really sure on that one, what the story was there, all I know was that it was the last I knew of Israel on that trip. It was definitely time to get back to the US. I had veered way off the cliff.

I was overweight, and down in the dumps, I had to do whatever it took to get the pounds off, and get myself up off the ground. Even if it meant working at a Jewish summer camp in the middle of the woods somewhere.

Most people I knew who got jobs straight out of the highly respected Jewish Studies college I was studying at, were offered teaching positions in Jewish studies, I however, was given, was offered, or had chosen, take your pick, the dance teacher and choreographer position for over 400 little Jewish munchkins. I learned all the Israeli dances on one foot, because I forgot to mention they hired me to be the Israeli dance teacher, which I really knew a smidgeon of. I picked them up fairly quick and used my creativity, my love and passion for dance to inspire some original creations of art on the dance floor, and used the summer to get in rockstar magazine shape.

In the mornings, every morning for two months, I would wake up early and climb out of my cot, and pump some iron. Green plastic ones at that. They were responsible for some killer arms. I walked an hour everyday with intentions to melt away the blubber, AB routine, an effort to get a six pack, in the middle of the power walk, complete with a vehement arm swaying swing.

Every free moment I had I would spend in the dance studio, free-styling, visioning or choreographing for the kids. It was a turn of the century summer for me and my new bod. I walked into the interview, my first after college, and nailed it.

The director Joe was definitely thinking about nailing a few other things to the wall besides picture frames. I had to hand it to my dedication and commitment to health.

My first job was as a hostess, at a family joint called Goldendays
in upstate New York. This is where I was "sexually harassed" on the job for real. I was walking up or down the stairs of the place, to his

office or from his office who knows which, when

he grabbed thats right my arse. sweet ass as we

Americans like to say.

I zipped it, never said a peep, it was probably one

of the longest standing jobs I ever had. Plus, I

was very hot for the cook there. He made me the

juiciest meat, and boy did he have a sweet ass.

I became the huntress, knew what I liked, and

sometimes how to get it. Even if only for a while.

Now everything has changed. I have hung up my

arrow for a sweet spot on the couch. Relaxing like

a queen. I am ready for a true and sacred

partnership. Equal where we both feel equally as

lucky to have found each other at long last.

After fifteen years without a television, yes, you

heard me right, and no drugs to boot, I bought an

LED screen at Best Buy and some cable to go with it.

The first three weeks glued to the screen, and then to the reality station. Third grade projectional ego tripping phonies. So why in the world was I glued, mouth dropped open, staring at how we humans could be so raw and mean?

More specifically how could have I been that spiteful mean girl for a decade and then some. Awakening to my own hurts, wounds, healing, and pain. I ran up the mountain screaming at the demons screaming in my head.

In Austin, there was an Indian restaurant where I would go to eat dhal, soothing, cleansing dal, and sit in the airy, comfort of simplicity and beauty. Every so often they would have a weekend healer's fair. I had a friend that played around with energy healing and I decided to attend. There was a women there who drew pictures of peoples star spirits, the way their soul was seen in the god-sphere. She began drawing mine, the image was female and blue, and had stars all over her body. She told me her name was Astraya, and that one day I would meet someone who would be transmitting healing powers to me that were able to heal anyone from any dis-ease or illness. He was from another planet, and so was I. I thought this was one of the most bizarre things anyone could say to another, look them in the eyes, and mean every word they were saying. Somewhere, somehow I felt here words to be true, although my mind had a hard time believing in the how, in what format was this to occur, was this even possible?

We've all heard of a sleeping prophet, well a prophet at the least. Maybe one that was walking around. Drinking coffee. Or tea. I was always the tea drinker. Never understanding why folks went crazy about coffee. What was it about coffee that people drank in dove into the stores for? Until someone mentioned she uses it to keep her regular, an excuse she said. Wow, I thought maybe America uses coffee to keep them regular.

This was an entirely new concept to me at age thirty-five, when my body was telling me it needed this information. If you catch my drift, yes, I was in the dark about the ways in which people kept their bowels regular, while exploring the esoteric wisdom and ideas of Kabbalah, Zen Tantric Buddhism, Native American shamanism, Chinese Medicine, philandering about from one religion, philosophy to the next. I was galavanting around, and was in most cases in great shape, up and down the yoyo spin of emotional eating, and now age catching up with me.

I learned about this coffee phenomena rescue remedy system from a child's mother I met one day sitting at a gelato shop. She was nine, brilliant, very mature, and reminded of myself when I was grade four. Her name was Katerina, and I confided to her mother about my coffee dilemma, after her daughter and I discussed what books we were reading and had just read, some of her artwork, and how she had raised one hundred dollars to send to help Haiti, the people suffering from a natural disaster there, who had lost their homes and some their lives, her mother being adopted, and what we thought the root of her origins were. Her father was Jewish, and she had a brother who had Down Syndrome who was six years old.

We formed a bond, a friendship, all of us that continued through many lunches, Christmas Eve dinners, which eventually ended in disaster and heartache, and my gaining another fifteen pounds I had worked furiously and hard to lose. I felt great, Sonia was taking me out for my birthday. As I had taken her and her husband out the week before. From the get go the young, handsome waiter and I had some chemistry, and she was flailing about in a jealous frenzy. Very surprising. She starting throwing out jab after jab in jealous attack on many different issues and topics, using information I had trusted her with, which I was far from expecting, after telling me about all of her female friendships. I did not have many friends at the time, she knew this and so I was a bit envious of her relationships she had kept and met up with for girlfriends retreats months over the last ten years of her life or more. She must have punched

me all of my body emotionally, and after lunch I
was fully throttled, felt betrayed to a woman I trust
opened my heart to, and was ready to end the
relationship immediately.

Sometimes we implode, and sink into a
depression, sometimes we explode and lash out
at the world for injustice and mistreatment. Either
way we are mistreating ourselves in the process.
We must learn to notice the rate and internal
working of our interior.

My saving grace has been a gift directly from the white
brotherhood of light, the angels, or what some might call the
realms of the fifth dimension, who have shared with me, I am
one of them. A channel, a direct messenger, a mouthpiece for
the gods, the Maker. The energies.

A channel, he or she has been sent as one who will aid
many to come to a better understanding of their relationships

with their Creator and their relationships to other people. People come with the knowledge that yes this man or woman has been in the presence of their Maker. They have seen the visions of those expanses we all seek-to pull the veil aside that we may peer into the future. Psychic is soul seeing, seeing is soul. Psychic is that of the Maker. The gift bestowed upon those that have been in the Presence of.

My new teacher Ashoto, was a Tibetan master from the heavens, who spoke through a human being named Boris. The man that the seer in Austin had predicted I would meet, had come to pass. He was transmitting his vision and knowledge, all of what is sacred over to his new devoted student, daughter, and friend.

Return to the Sacred

Who decides what is sacred? What does it mean to be revered?

What does it mean to be treasured or held high? The ecstatic bliss we yearn for is found in the revered. The quest for love is through the tunnel of reverence. This interconnected union with our inner nature and unity of community is the gateway to love. Loving through compassion is the great gateway to joy. Joy is the vital ingredient to make the dough rise, to allow divine presence to enter and stay.

Reverence is an ancient virtue that survives among us in half forgotten patterns of civility, in moments of inarticulate awe, and in nostalgia for the lost ways of traditional cultures. We have the word, reverence in our culture, but scarcely know how to use it.

This happens when something is revered, cherished, cared for, holy in one's eyes yet not another. Life.

A sacred journal of ones thoughts, a meal someone has worked hard to prepare, a life of an orphan child struggling to survive in Africa with AIDS.

This may also be seen in examples such as placing value on and cherishing the flowers growing out of a cement walkway, as someone at the same moment steps upon them without a second glance. Similarly, this occurs when one values one life over another. The deep irreverence found in warfare. Killing without regard to the sacred essence of life force. Killing the sacred before it is revealed and found.

Irreverence is the disregarding of all creation as love, as a blessing, and regarding it rather as a curse donned to muddle through. It is when life itself is seen as a burden one must bear as opposed to a gift given and bestowed upon.

The reverence of wisdom is through the transmission of the grandmothers. The connection to other through sacred ritual allows for the bonding and sharing between men and women of all ages. The intergenerational gaps that have formed are far too large to leap across and safely make it over onto the other side. The fear of what will come, and the crone wisdom have been placed out of reach. Crones have become invisible, resulting in the reverence of an inauthentic self. We can bring back our grandmothers and their wisdom in this day, by coming together, as one body, one living, breathing goddess soul that we are.

We can ignore the behest of the grandmothers, only at extreme peril, for theirs are the powers not only of the past and the present, but also of the future.

The truest symbol of the future is the one our society avoids. If we are to survive, it is the divine we must fully honor.

The grandmothers are calling us, calling us to form an outer and inner circle that is the web of life, honoring the sacred. This outer circle of elders forms an elder council, the protective, wise shell of the pod that weathered the storms and lived to tell their stories. They provide the lining that is necessary for the inner circle to take shape, the young pea in the pod, needing nurturance, reassurance, guidance, and reflection.

When my grandmother lit the candles with me for the first time, I saw all of my ancestors bringing in the holy Divine Feminine through the light of the flame, burning, burning with wisdom and compassion…burning for remembrance, burning for life.

Blessed to have been raised by both grandmothers since birth. The grandmothers have in many ways taken on the role of mother, as well as the one who has truly seen and heard me in all my many faces and guises. In looking at my family lineage, the womb of Mother Russia that held my grandmothers and their goddess statues is the birthing matroyshka doll, where you will find another generation of dolls in each womb.

This is a symbol for transmission of tradition as well as trauma and memory, hidden and revealed. For the stories were held in secret, as much of many Russian Jewish family's history was washed away by the Nazis, by the suitcase holding images of ancestry that was stolen while en route to the U.S., in our case via Italy, are both gone forever.

The stories were buried in the rubble of the war, and the shattering of the vessels, of psyche, body, and soul. From the womb, where both my mother and father were born and came from, came the emergence of my destiny.

The dance of life started inside of the womb, while you were doing the water dance of the spiral, inside womb space, holy of holies, creation--the sacred ritual container for birthing, the sacred waters which cleanse and purify, and then bleed in mourning and rebirth.

The dance of life continues through the transmission of life force.

When one life dance ends, another ensues. The entering and exiting of a dance in sacred circle, whom are you next to, connected to, glancing at, at one with? When you dance individually, when do you begin? Are you standing or on the ground, is your dance choreographed or improvisational? Who is your director, are you a marionette? Who pulls your strings? How do we receive our wisdom and knowledge? How do we decide which step to put forward, and which direction to go? Whom to follow? Who will lead? Are we alone, or in community? Is there an audience? Are we on stage?

There was on stage again. At thirty-five, without a pot to piss in, I started small. Some back country joint. Hired anyone who came in. Perfect Practice scenario I thought, and without a license I did not have to take my top off yet, I would build up to it. Mainly I was thinking about how was I going to put gas into my car, an old one, and get some damn stripper shoes. I had to borrow the money for those.

I had never spent any time at all in an establishment such as the one I was going to bare my soul in, not really. I had some semblance of confidence under my belt, just not in the naked performance sense.

I had done a one women show in the past, and had been a ballroom dancer in college, on the dance team.

I coveted the Mexican engineer as a partner. He was the best dancer and the salsa king. Salsa became a way of escape for me. Passionate waves of movement I lost myself to the undulations of the dance.

He was not interested until I was interested in him sexually, then all hell broke loose.

I went to Mexico with him.

Asked for a little girl, and poof there I was pregnant at age 20.

Still dating my first love Eli, from Croatia, the island of Dalmatia to be exact. It was a betrayal a deeply disturbing betrayal of something I valued and cherished, he was thousands of miles away, and I was starting to re-member. I was starting to feel betrayed and the rage inside of me was sent into forms of actions even I, certainly I did not understand at the time.

How could I done this to him us, looking back I see it was a repeat performance of what my mother did behind the back of my father. I wanted to re-create to heal it, re-member, it, I was an infant that saw, felt, and heard everything in my crib.

Soaked in all the per-verbal ugliness, hatred, horror, and despair of a young mother seduced, betrayed herself, and yearning for a better life.

Eli did love me however, more than anyone I have ever known. I continued to dream of Eli for the next fifteen years. My mother told me I would never find anybody that loved me as much as Eli did. He would come to me, the gorgeous Adonis that he was, soft, sweet and kind, a brilliant genius, taught me so many things, about so many things.

He was a warrior, that took me to a war. The SCA war was held every year, in Pennsylvania, where 10,000 people gathered to reenact the Renaissance. I was thrilled. The best part was seeing my man robed up in various costumes, including real armor before he went off to battle on a horse. Yes, really. There was nothing like it. Before after, or since. Until I met my love mate for life. Paul. The warrior of all warriors, going to battle for his own life each day.

I had an abortion after Mexico. It was the secret the catalyst that changed my life then.
Now sixteen years later on birth control for the first time, and 3 abortions later, I wonder if the backwards breech theory really does hold true.

I got up on the stage in my boot and let it rip, I had no idea about what I was really doing exactly, but I had to make a dollar. There and then I learned the value of a dollar. It took me thirty-five years to do it, but I had finally succeeded.

I worked my way around, and got the hang of being on stage and the rhythm and flow of this new kind of dance. One for food, gas, and survival. A very different kind of dance.

One day, one of the dancers said I was not even close to being high maintenance of the Foxy Resort, a club in downtown Atlanta, by then I had followed my teacher Dallas across the country from Austin. I pulled into town with a few dollars saved up in my pocket just to make it there, and rent a room. A stale pizza on the front seat of my Red BMW.

She said I would never make it there and was not cut out for that kind of crowd. Little did she know my destiny was scheduled to spearhead my arrows in cupid's way, dropping me right smack dab in the middle of the place. Before I did, I decided to move up a notch and get my feet a little bit salty and sweet, more like learn how to be nasty enough to make it work well.

I heard I did not belong in a club, and stood out like a sore thumb man a times, did not bother me at all. I heard I looked likes someone who was just there as a challenge. The light in the dark beams bright. It was the battle of the light and the dark at every turn.

I walked into a club call Glam Girls the next day, and auditioned for a beautiful women with black diamonds in her ears, hair pulled back into a French twist, she must have been around my age. She had been dancing for the last fifteen years, and was now the new manager of Glam, a middle of the road club, certainly more intriguing than the first stop on my list. I was a newbie to say the least. I told her this was my first time dancing and asked her if she would teach me the ropes. She said sure, and answered a few questions.

She said, it was just like a regular 9 to 5 job, with regular customers, she had built up over the years. Tamara, told me to go to the room next door and practice on the pole before my audition. So I did.

This club was enormous and had three stages. It was glamtastic. Was I at thirty-five? There happened to be a man who pulled into the parking lot at the same time I did. He was in the audience at 2 p.m. The only one there, and began wilding screaming and throwing money on the stage as I began to move. Tamara said I was definitely hired, and I thanked god for watching over me and sending this random fellow who was probably high on cocaine my way. I got the job. Now how I the world was I going to fill it, and make some money, fast?

After a very short time at Glam, I had made some mistakes, big ones, but was a quick study, and never made the same mistake again, namely going home with the biggest drug dealer in California and his partner, as well as having gotten into a few cat fights withe girls. This was going to be harder than I thought. I was up for the challenge, but I had to move on. I had learned enough at the two clubs to feel confident enough to step up again. I remembered the club Tamara had mentioned while we spoke, the one she had spent all her years at, and decided that hers was the next stop. As it turns out, it was the very same club the dancer at the first club said I was not cut out for. I knocked on the door the next day, had an audition, and somehow got the job.

Real breasts and all, I was an anomaly. When I started making all the money, did not do drugs, or sell my body fro sex, yet I top dog, and was raking in the cash. At a certain point after many cat fights, the literal twisting of a dancer's arm, my twisting hers after she spoke some words about me in front of the owner, some glue up the hole of my locker's lock, I had had enough and retired after six months of dancing the money dance. I was burned out. Saved up, and done with the darkness and the underground life once and for all. I was out.

The tall blonde girl at the silent meditation retreat came to mind, as I was wrapping up my days dancing, she had told me she was going to be a stripper 8 years back, and I was stunned shocked, appalled by her disclosure back then. She said she was going to drive truck as well. All of which she was going to do in a different way, she said. A sacred way, I say.

Everything I did was for god.

Tamara showed up at the club, her haunt, her old stomping grounds a few months later, turns out she quit her job as manager over at Glam and was now back on the set, only to find her new hire, the top seller on the red hot market, perverts row and it's perimeters. She was seething with jealousy, and began to make fun of the way I danced while I was on stage. It was not long before she was hinting at her plans to oust me out of the club in one way or another. I got the message soon enough and did not want to be the brunt of her insecurities, for we were now playing in the dark big leagues of the underground and the stakes were high.

I finally owned my own home, a gift entrapment from my mother, paid off in cash, but that was all. So that is where dancing for money came into play.

I had always known that one day I would become

a stripper, never at thirty-five years old, but

somewhere in the depths of my soul I knew I had

this house, and had exhausted all my resources.

The time was now to break free my the chains

and shackles of my mother's reign and control. It

was time. I was willing to do anything to take care

of myself. Besides working a 9 to 5 that is, been

there done that, its like choking on stale sausage.

I would rather be dancing. At times I hated it, it

made me feel so low, and other times I felt like a

walking million dollar queen bee.

Strong, secure, wanted, beautiful, and sexy.

Coming home with a wad of cash that I had

made. I learned the value of a dollar.

Knowing the sacred. The way is the knowing.

Follow your own path, your own voice.

Only you know your way to your own sacred.

I found my way to my sacred lover right after I

had lunch at the Indian restaurant. I walked into

to his office, and he passed me in the hallway. I

thought I was seeing a mirage, literally. I could

not believe my eyes. Was he even real I thought?

I felt my etheric body fall to the floor. He may be.

We'll find out. I was already in a great mood, for

some unknown reason, and as we know hot for

someone, but who. I followed his business

partner into his office and kept staring into the

office next to me, I could not keep focused on the

conversation at hand, my eyes and heart did not

stop glancing to see if he was in his office.

 Paul.

I waved coyly, he made me feel like a woman. A

strong, sweet, sensitive, sexy woman. He was

stronger than me, and then I looked deep into his blue eyes, he came from the stars, where we originally met, were destined, and bonded... all time literally spun and stood still at the very same moment.

On our first date he summed up my childhood and mostly my future, Who was I to become in this lifetime, what was my mission, and why were we here. So, your a leader, and a teacher, he said, after asking me what games I played as a child.

He told me he was part Native and from a ranch in Montana at dinner, sushi, a white ornately planned and pinned space, elegant, with people shouting in the party wings, I was in heaven, felt like I was on a ship, a cruise ship, a space, ship, who knew.

All I knew was that I was in heaven.

_ Sacred Love_____

I want to wake up with you and the dawn

I want to hold your hand all night long

The love we share is so rare

I love you all through my heart

I love you longing while we are apart

I want to kiss your belly

I want to look up at you while you kiss mine

I love you I love you I love you

_____ *Face to face.*

To turn towards me you must pull away from her

Away from an enmeshed situation that blocks your flow

Of love to another, your mate, your soulmate to be exact

One who has been waiting for you…and searches to find you

Who searched until you are found…it all comes round

For it all begins with a kiss, a lust, a longing

For connection of soul and spirit, for the waters make us blend

and bleed

Caress the sides of cheeks … in turn we must play the game

by their rules

The faucets squeak and let out a sound of harmless peep

Sound waves chime in…the light of the siren, as it rings night

Morning wakens to the fall of dimly lit window sills

Calling the bitter ones away from love.

Your soul stands in line to receive the fanciful contraption,

contraction.

Constriction of the worlds light in vain

She processes the wisdom sent forth from

The loins of the womb-face= baby-face, loving womanhood

No more, all in all is a mystical serene dream to prevent all

from coming down

Journeying downwards from serendipitous consternation

She unveils your true depths of constance

In light of preventive measure and medicines he will call to her

mother earth to come By the side of the road

By the side of his bed, by the side of his heart.

———

Silent Passions.

The wisps of the moons crescent catches the corner of my eye,

and the strand of hair in yours. I brush back and run my fingers gently through your hair, leading down your face, caressing gently, then neck, as I blow and whisper sweet nothings in your ear.....I call you to come forth in wonderment and mystery to please me...

As the moon shines down on my back you watch me undress slowly...

I embody the goddess dancing elegantly, gracefully like the gazelle, and you that know that you have been waiting to protect and honor your virgin bride come....

You watch with anticipation and gaze at the spirit within.

My nipples rise as I see you harden, elevate....

My veil covers, as I unveil myself to you....

Slowly, you come up to join me from the bed and caress my face with your large muscular yet smooth palms and look me deep in the eyes and tell me what you would like with them..i

I know and hear all you want and you sense my knowing…

You begin to kiss my earlobes and neck, my back, spontaneously moving in all directions.

I do not know where you will go next, you keep me guessing….kissing and caressing my nipples you pick me up and carry me to the bed, where candles flicker parallel with the moon's rays reflecting inner light that is external.

You then bring me to the bathtub with sacred light, and rose petals, and flowers everywhere, it smells of sensual aromas… as you yearn to climb inside of me and the large whirlpool..and begin to caress all of me and kiss every inch of my skin, warm and wet, listening to exotic silky smooth music, and sipping an exotic love potion...

We then dance towards the soft luxurious rug where I love you with a feather all over and rub you gently with my lips and palms…

I blindfold you and begin to tease you until no end, until you are begging me to make love to you…but no wait then your remember to please me first…

You begin to take out the massage oil, and begin to sensuously, slowly, gently yet firm, rub all of me, beginning with my belly, and down my thighs, you remember my breasts, and my toes, my hands, and fingers, and my clitoris…you gently touch, and tease me as with my breasts, you tingle and tease, and tizzle…..me with your tongue….not forgetting my moth needs to be tizzled as well….

Then you flip me over by placing one hand underneath my body and creatively get on top of me oiling and kissing, caressing the rest of me...

Once you have poured out all of your love onto the backside, you begin to flip me back over and pour chocolate syrup in my love nest and begin devouring her, delicately….licking and worshipping her…

I love to be teased and you know exactly how and when to begin to bring me up to sit with you, looking into each others eyes, we breathe in unison, and begin to merge into union with one another…equal lovers and partner honoring and respecting the depth within.

Harmonics of Wholeness.

The way a seed grows in a pot-knowing there is room for all seedlings to plant their roots.

The individual has room for exploration into their freedom just as the seed has room to plant it roots and flow into their own process.

If they run into each other it is okay, there is no competition for there is room for all and all have the same essence.

The meeting of roots, meeting of souls...

The Intelligence of each soul center, holds a temple of energy, it is the power to heal each organ within the body. We have the power to heal ourselves.

We have and hold the divinity within our own bodies, our own energy wisdom.

These temples of energy wisdom hold all of our souls knowing.

The Harmonics of wholeness lie in the roots and depths of soul knowing, by being in relationship with our deepest heart.

The trees sing, to each other and vibrate their knowing through energy, we access our own inner knowing through the beauty of wholeness that lives in the basin of our heart strings, they are pulled when there is something to be said. They are speaking to us through a melody of dis-ease and or sorrow. We must heed their call. The second chakra might be weeping as the weeping aspen tree, orange in color, weeping for the suffering of mother earth and all the suffering she has endured.

The dead and dying and those that were shedding or that have shed their skin, were sharing their innate wisdom with us. Aspen body wisdom is an undeniable one. They stand naked in their stark beauty, their eyes revealed to see and be seen. Their power and resiliency to move on and through the fire they hold within their own bodies, the fire and sunlight they hold underneath their skin.

They hold a wisdom of wholeness that reaches into their symbiotic relationship with the pine trees that hold their shadow by showing us their light, the pine trees cycle of succession as the light of the aspen trees fade to allow for the dark cycle to enter, as in all of our lives. We must surrender to the cycles within our lives-living, growing, dying, transforming, flowing into and out of the pain we are receptacles for…we move toward the light as we gaze at the waters, clear, pure, reflecting our inner truth of light being. We in turn resonate with both the dark and light within our being, the spiritual within the physical body, the physical within the spiritual realms, the soul that resides in our body temples.

We are the dying aspens, we are the weeping orange ones, we are the ones shedding our skin, and the water that shows us the truth of the purity of our souls. We are one with the infinite sun, we are the aspens that teach us to live amongst our inner fires, rising from the flames and grow from their wisdom. The trees are singing their wisdom knowing into my wisdom knowing.

Whispering into yours.

Landscapes of the heart, fashion a wardrobe that allows for transcendence amongst the bravest of today's warriors. When the interconnectedness of Self is explored on multiple levels, the ego becomes selfless and wanes as the moon. Empowering women and men alike to take social action; action in the way of acting from the heart.

My message is one of the heart. In essence creating a picture of an interconnected world, where boundaries are limited in the face of war and destruction. We are in a time where we must open our hearts and feel, as we would with our human lovers. The intimacy of living in the world as if you are in constant connection and interconnection with the Universe and each other.

This is the landscape by which we must clothe ourselves in and create a new consciousness around. Whereby we design each piece of clothing with the intention of oneness. This oneness is what I call "soul love." This oneness is one of the main points she brings to the reader in the World as Lover, Lover as Self. Issues of self, and how we as a society are inherently responsible for each other and each other's well being, as we are all interconnected, and one with the earth, and universe.

As a result, we must reach out to each other, and create from a similar fabric, as we are all woven from the same breath.

I believe it is the warrior women in today's society, who are bringing home these ideas. Living from and with heart, and in compassion, and calling many to action, and to living in oneness.

A poignant concept which spoke to my heart revolves around compassion and insight used as weapons. They are able to be used in dismantling massive weapons of destruction, as well as weapons of the heart. Although one shared purpose is of peeling away the layers of the love onion in the world. This translates to transforming the one we currently live in, into one filled with eyes that are able to see love in all others.

All may be nourishing and delicious to our palette is we have the eyes to see. This impulse is the heart throbbing of the universe, of the Creatrix, Goddess, of the bridal mystics who gave us a glimpse into what yearning for connection, and in essence creation is about. This yearning for love and wholeness masks and disguises itself in the robes of many, cars, or addictive tendencies of artists and spiritualists who have not yet awakened to their inner power and beauty.

To move in the world as your lover is a spiritual practice we could all embrace to release the power our own desperation which has held us in our own prison, looking at the world as a battlefield or trap. This is opposed to dancing with the darkness and in, sweet play, rasa-lila, an outburst of love, reminiscent of eroticism.

Last night I was reminded how healing it was to play. To remind myself of my sweet essence in the interplay and spontaneous performance jam I was a part of. We babbled, sang gibberish opera, moved in shapes and stillness, and heard one another' sweet melodic songs of soul. This night was intimate, erotic, nourishing in many ways. It was truly allowing for my inner warrior to express herself as the glorious sunshine and light that hides amongst the clouds at times.

Home Follows.

Crawling into spaces that are too small for you

Read between the lines, mystery calmer, intrigue of the century

I sense your presence in the shell of life dreams, butterfly

cream

Fading princess power queen mold overlay

Doing his dance in drum stance,

 Rain form spirit, mind, heart connection

You see me as beautiful you see your reflection

Evaporating ego, mind tart heart of the core mountain lines.

Who is the maiden here walking along castle ledge amidst

clouds wandering

Vessels breaking the core to climb onto larger surface faces of

the one

Mirror reflection of light cornered to revere inner serenity pieces

of peace

Shine within windows allowing sand to seep through pores of

holiness

Together at last we pray for the unfolding to enlighten our

lives

Our breath that pulls us near to center, holds the space to climb

into ' the pot

That was empty, now so full, overflowing onto the ledge of the

counter space

Colored purple with heart of angels transparent as they let you

feel their pain and truth, Covering shades of green trunk

shrunken rage as red safety and protection now

I see, doing our dance to shells of life that crawl with home,

everywhere is home now

Anywhere I am, home follows.

On the broomstick of change, I love the rain as it is here

I love the sun as it is near-now, what is here now is now

There is no future and past, a bygone of today

In my love for you I feel the suns rays

I feel your smile and meet your pace

Within my heart I hold your face in my prayers and trace the

lines I will come to know

As the presence I met then when all was gone and shed upon

To bring about

A land of love. To stand and speak the truth above in our time,

we love.

You will be here to face the rain in time I know, we will share

the dance.

Carefree without pain the centerfold of love, a cradled world of

transcendental gain.

NO smoking, NO talking, decorates the door; He thinks it was a joke, yet it was in all seriousness, the doorkeeper said," it's fourteen dollars sir..and this is a no talking show. The reality of setting the sacred space sinks in as this music woven in the mystical nature of silence, begins. In between the spaces, allowing for all vibration to be felt and heard.

The first spoken sound we hear is moaning…

The "Grey Saw" is all about the red. Raw, bloody, and all about the heart. The music that was given birth to was a reflection of the Grey Saw that Monday night on the North side of Chicago, Al Capone's old favorite, hosting a bluesy jazz combo.

Within the spaces, presence is cultivated, the audience is able to hear the nuances of the dark and light attunement of their own soul, while allowing the soul of the music to flow through them. Both band members and audience were mesmerized by the created magic between them, a combination of trance and mindfulness. Ready for steady love riding the waves of wonder, amazement, and awe. The drummer goes wild and loses his drum stick, the audience mirrors his frenzy, shown in head bobbing trance dance. A blind man's feat, never missing a beat, just as the heart continues in steady love, the river flows out onto the crowd immersed in CO-creation. What is hidden in recorded music, streams live as the oceans waves pulse with life?

The heartbeat of the elements ring clear in ears opening in hearts desire, sensual and sultry, vocals line fire, earth, water, and air. Watching the voice of love making waves flow through the band members, and audience, dialoging in dance, physically stationary, while spirits flow and merge in present time.

Then there is the past, watching over us. The ancient, is lit amongst the sea of red, white Athenian Goddess stands tall and proud. She is the voice that is being heard tonight. The silent warrior, protectress, bearer and holder of a cauldron of voices of wisdom, holds the space. She is seemingly out of place, she is in exile, she yearns to be the voice in the silence, being heard. She is the one who mesmerizes the audience, and is the divine inspiration for the performer, she stands with and behind them in solidarity, for our solo and collective voices being heard.

To be able to hear, it is necessary to be very quiet, to listen respectively—

That is, if we wish to permit facts, point of view, personal truth, to tell us their truth, we must learn to listen to them in a very specific way—silently, hushed, quietly, fully listening, non-interfering, receptive, patient, respectful of the matter-at-hand, courteous to the matter-in-hand.

I became a mother at age 10. Got my period, starting wearing pink lipstick, and for all intensive purposes started raising my brother Bradley Mark. They asked me for a name. That stated with B. First name that came to mind was Brad, the boy I had a crush on at the moment. I was in fourth grade.

He was the most popular boy in school, and they liked the name. They wanted to come up with a name to honor the step-horrors father, his name was Max by the way, it was his father whose name began with B. My own mother's name was Disa, but she went by the Americanized version of Dolores.

Dolores, was about thirty-six when she had Bradley, had another c-section, and immediately fell ill, with a blood clot in her left leg. She was bed ridden. I was rising, up to the challenge, of motherhood. Was I ready? Um, sure, it seemed god though I had what it took to stay up at night, feed the little bugger, and sing sweet lullabies to him before I was off to grade 4 every morning.

Bradley was a very sweet child, smart, and followed directions well. I terrorized him for a few moments, with a small musical black and white wind up doll in my room I called Clowny, inflicting some sort of terror into his tiny life. I loved him very much. I treasured his preciousness, and showed him the kind of love that was offered to me. Mixed motions of love, torture, terror and hate.

My pure soul came out mainly in my music. My songs, I sang for him. My touch, as I rocked him, and soothed him. Soothing my own child self at the same time.

I never had a childhood. The pictures of me show

me white as a ghost, a sheet at the morgue.

Dressed in red.

All the blood drained out of my face.

Where was I? Must have been hell.

I tried to escape the black wooden rectangle box

of a house as much as I could. I had a best friend

named Cassie who lived down the street on

Chestnut Drive. She had a blended family, they

were much wealthier than us, and traveled often,

to interesting places such as Killington, NY for

skiing, and their summer house a few hours

away. All other times I would find myself in my

room or in the basement.

I was kept a "princess" in the ways of my not being allowed to mow the lawn, or do the dishes. Ever.

Somehow they managed to allow me to do my own laundry when I became a mother. The one household chore I seem to enjoy and appreciate doing for myself, and others.

People always asked me how I ate, which was a preposterous question in my mind. I went to he store, ate out, had others cook for me, I placed, or stuffed food into my mouth, how else do people eat I thought. My claim to fame or failure was the fact that I did not cook. Well, I ate out of cans and cereal boxes for the most part, except for the traditional Russian meals at events, parties, and my grandmothers house. The women were notorious for cooking, thick, long lasting meals that soothed the soul, animal soul that is, and extended the stomach and hips.

I was a chubby child.

He, Max, the horror, cut my hair short like a boy, and my mothers when I was in the fourth grade. Sometimes I would have nightmares that he was in Israel about to cut my long hair off.

That is were my memories started coming back to me again. I was far enough, across the world, to feel safe enough in my own mind, skin, never mind the fear of being blown to smithereens on a daily basis, I was no longer in the line of fire of Max and Dolores and the world of a prison of contempt. Their wrath was a black chord of succulent poison, that would wrap it's death grip around every inch of my skin and invade any semblance of sanity love that was left there after 23 years of corporal punishment.

I felt like a princess when I was with Paul, he was the fantasy of a warrior that would protect and honor me, make me melt and scream to the core.

He mentioned his childhood in Montana, on a Native American reservation and his initiations into the clan.

The tests, the wounding, the struggle, the humiliations, the outsider looking in.

I mentioned briefly a time at George's place in LA, when I was sleeping on the floor after having spent some time at Ike's Santa Barbara beach house to Paul. Speaking only of a dream I had had.

As it turned out my former fiancé, Ike, was sleeping with me, enjoying it thoroughly, but calling his girlfriend Sarai, on the phone downstairs after was just had some very erotic sex.

I overheard the conversation, and felt the poisonous betrayal shooting through my veins. My sweet trusting Jewish nun like tendencies were out the window and right out onto Ike. We were done. I had him drive me two and a half hours back to LA, had nowhere to go, except an Orthodox Jews house, whom I had just met the night before, named George. He said, I could stay with him for several days until I found a place to go. That was the beginning of a seven year friendship. Love ship. Definitely not a sex ship.

Most of my closest relationships were formed in a period of crisis when someone decided to have my back and it often times revolved around home. Having a place to stay, a roof over my head.

A few years after that, I had flown in to LA for a brief stay with George. I had a potential job interview somewhere in the Hollywood Hills. I woke up one morning, and started screaming none other than the words, Montana, it's a ranch in Montana. I saw the ranch and really had never had such an outburst before about any of my dreams. It was loud and profound. I had absolutely no idea what it meant. I did have an inkling that my man was going to be from Montana, and of course I was obsessed on my search for that man, and if Montana was a clue

that brought me that much closer to my dream of

finding my love mate, I was going to get to the

bottom of it, even if it meant asking each person

that even mentioned Montana, to dig a little

deeper to see if there was any possible

connection to this dream and my own love

fantasies.

Well, I did have some close calls of course. I

started talking to a man in Hawaii while I was

living in California, still trying to get Ike fully out of

my addiction veins, cause frankly that was some

good sex. Disrespectful and degrading in all

senses of the word, except for in the actual

bedroom. He was a surfer, and surfers now how

to ride the waves of mother earth. In addition he

played the guitar and sang songs to me, which I

have always loved. In reality he used and abused

me for sex just like when I was four.

The other side of Paul was that he was MR.

Genius Intuitive, Techy Sex Geek. The sexiest

geek I ever met. He read my mind, and kissed me

in a way that made me feel like he was kissing

every part of my body mind, and soul as he

placed his juicy wet lips on mine.

Paul touched my neck inside of his black and

silver metallic army truck, as some women, was

banging on the back of it, mixing the fear, surprise

pleasure pain, I was immediately turned on, he

said, "that turned you on,?in amazement, and I

replied, "wasn't it meant to"? he said, "I think we

are going to dance well together."

"Yes, I thought, 'I couldn't agree with you more.'

I could not wait to dance with Paul. On the dance floor. In the bedroom, everywhere. When I asked Paul to go dancing with me, he said he had not been dancing in a long time, and needed to take a lesson and brush up.

He lifted me out of the truck, like a princess, someone who deserved to be carried, lifted out from under the rubble of a life she had lived through. When he stepped out of the truck to find the cause of the shaking, I had never felt so safe. He was going to take care of it, and me.

Paul and I started talking everyday on the phone, and as things started moving along, and I started feeling closer to him, I also started receiving strange signs that he was seeing other woman, but that was way out of my beliva-sphere. I realized that I was not the only princess, in his

life.

It was not only he who was psychic.

Dumbfounded, newly insecure and in a quandary.

How could this all be happening at the same

time?

Besides these strange calls and coincidences,

and my intuition, I was in the middle of selling my

house, an investment property, and I had just

found out I was closing in three days.

He was on a business trip, and had called me

minutes after the news came in, and I was in a bit

of a fucked up panic in that moment, reminiscent

of times past, when I did not have a place to live,

except for the fact that I was about to become a

very rich woman. Rich in my mind, anyway. I

could go and stay anywhere, and do anything I

wanted, I wanted to be with him.

I was looking for love the real true love, and

would not settle for anything less.

He did know how to cook. He invited me

over to his house for dinner one night. I had the

gate code, and made my way in. He was selling

some tires and so I waited patiently. I had a few

gift baskets for him and his father for Easter in the

passenger seat. His hands were all grimy from

the tar of the tires, and said he would help me

carry them in after he washed his hands.

I had filled his basket with my favorite books,

crystals, chakra love spray, Godiva chocolate and

avocado soap for his travel trip, home, office, and

his father's basket with golf and the mind books,

two subjects I knew he would love.

He brought me a gift too. It was a free month of yoga in his neighborhood. In case I was ever at his house. Super sweet and thoughtful, and what a great sweaty aide to stay in shape and focused.

There were times when he felt my love, my unconditional love for him. Yes, he was handsome, yes he was wealthy, as he alluded to, and yes he was intelligent and sexy, but when I sent him my love in many ways and forms, he knew and felt it. It was if there was no denying pure true love, sent from the stars and my heart.

He said a few times that he had never felt something like it before. He was not ready for a commitment. That was clear.

Two months later, I was in a large bookstore, guided to stand in front of the bestseller shelf when a book fell off the shelf, and I just stood there in amazement, always wondering if that eerie event would ever happen to me. After being what most would call in the "woo woo" world for over fifteen years, I had never had a book fall to my feet from the angels as a message to read it. Here it was happening to me. After I closed my mouth from its hang open stance, I hunkered down, a word I learned from a very savvy six year old girl many years back. I picked up the paperback best seller off the shelf, the last in a trilogy. I read the back still in disbelief. I quickly placed it back on the shelf and walked out. How and why could that have been meant for me to read. Well, I had a feeling it was to do with Paul, but I decided to do some research on the book before buying it.

I went home and looked up the full description online. Yes, I was definitely meant to read it, and

it most certainly had to do with my relationship
with Paul.

Now that it was "over" for the last two months,
and had not heard even a peep from Paul, I was
wondering why in the world I had to read it and
why?

Was he coming back into my life through a book?
Was I going to read it and keep the hope alive,
would I understand him more?

The book was a love story, of a light and dark
erotic nature which dealt with dark sexual play
and power.

I decided to go to the bookstore and buy the
book. Well, I sped to the closest store in town
where I could get my hands on it. I could not find
the bestseller section, so I asked for the book by

name, and the teller said oh yes we have it right here. For the first time of my life a bit of embarrassment swept over me. It was unexplainable, until I started reading it. I could not put it down. I savored every page, and then raced through it. Each word reminding me of Paul. I jumped into the pages and the passion, dreaming of what it would be like to have him back in my life, our reunion, and reconnection.

After I finished the apparent pseudo women's porn, everywhere I turned, the news, people in the streets were all discussing this book that had fallen at my feet the day before.

What I did know was that he was in the ballroom dance club in college as well, and danced with his first wife every week when they first got together. Although he revealed to me that they could not dance together well.

He said he was hard to love. I knew different. I knew he would stay a bachelor, and a playboy until he met his best friend, someone, something real that he shared, and belonged to. Someone who maybe reminded him of his mother, but someone who reminded of himself, the female version, one the was the missing part of his soul.

His love mate.

I believe Paul knew that I was the one he had been waiting for his whole life. How could he not feel it, he even admitted feeling something when he saw me in the hall? The night before I met Paul, I had a dream that a blonde woman was handing me a baby boy. She looked like Meryl Streep. The night before we met, Paul was in LA meeting with a former actress that had blond hair.

He wanted a baby, children and definitely a boy. I did not know any of that but did share my dream with him. Why hide it, I was shocked with it myself.

A little sign, missing pieces, clues. Then I pulled a tarot card that I had never seen before, a Native American looking woman with long black hair by some water holding a swaddled child that said mothering at the bottom a week later.

Paul told me that he was going to retire in Montana or Minnesota on a ranch and have a Bed and breakfast, he said I could massage the women while he went hunting with the men. That was interesting as I wanted to have a retreat center for the last ten years. What a coincidence. I think not.

I wore my red heels on the days, I wanted to play red at the strip club, when my huntress hungary ways got the best of me, when I wanted to play with fire, or power. I would slap those heels on the stage this way and that way, getting the attention of those that sought the hidden innocence I reeled them in with. It was all there, the fire vixen rocking porn queen and the four year old that wanted daddy back in the bedroom, all there in one twisted but healed little body ready to play her part. It did get me into a bit of trouble and pain, yet the sexpot fruit roll up of a girl was all woman.

If there were lesbians in the club it was like honey to a bee, something different, unusual unique, why not, another day another dollar. I would dance for anyone paying the gold. Some paid

seven hundred dollars to slap my ass in front of

their friends, and some paid seven hundred

dollars to just be with in my company. Paid my

taxes for the year in one hour.

Don't think I did not study up on how to be a great

stripper. I did, I read books, and memoirs, and

researched some more. I even found a woman

from London selling her secret success finds.

Little did I know once I was unleashed, and I was

in my element, I could have wrote five books on

stripping and many other erotic business tips.

After the Rain:

When the sun beats down on the pavement-the earth thirsting

The desert yearning to be fed, that is the soul yearning to pour

forth

Be cleansed of the pain it is endured and gathered.

To allow for the earth's cleansing, allow your inner rain to fall

Give it permission

Bowing Down

Bowing down to earth

Surrender, in the gaze of waking mist

Knowing in the unknown, security of void in bliss

Speaking whispers call me home to my souls palace of

mystical perception

She joins in the laughter, he calls for her hand

For they are destined to be one in this land…

Underneath the stars he awakens to touch her gaze, and

widens the trail they walk on…Blistering hot sensation,

revelations of nations.

The phoenix rising from the ashes, a life well spent on deepening deduction, wellness has crept into your being from fruitful efforts in concluding your misery…and so she shifts and changes, transforms her knowing into one of destiny, into one of truth and faith, remember, you knew it then and now, a matter of memory, and not losing yourself to what is forsaken.

Beauty and poverty wrap their wings
Around my waist forming a skirt of silk
Arms flailing in the winds of time
Timelessness bound together within
Inner dimensions

Beauty and poverty wrap their wings
Around my waist forming a skirt of silk
Arms flailing in the winds of time
Timelessness bound together within
Inner dimensions of the dance

She breathes into your heart and takes away the pain. She strengthens your will by allowing you to believe in your inner heart's chamber, flowing and pumping with blood.

Calling of the womb: returning to the mother of your soul's heart, the blood that speaks through your veins, I remember you, queen goddess who runs through the night, the one goddess who call me home.

Celebrating the end of suppression, disassociation, and ultimate humility

To take a rest from the road
Sleep inside the car ride journey of amnesty
To pardon the self that has fallen to rise

To run and return to wake in the light of transitory

Energy fields of luscious green underneath fluorescent

rainbow's edge

How do I tour the fields with you?

Your commentary speaks wide and true to my inner being

A home that I am in is resting within

Running to greet you in the mirror that holds love

Owning my inner beauty as one, as the prize I win for long

battles fought

To own the home I have built, to dwell in the sanctuary I have

made sacred

Blowing in the winds, raindrops pelt down the back of the

window, the

Blending of twisted souls is won, the car whizzes by he thinks

he will win that prize we allow him to pass and are grateful for

not trailing our ass, as we cruise slowly by enjoying.

His lie to himself that he will win if he drives and drives faster with more horsepower.

Jumping to catch the next vine, it is drinking the wine slowly next to the golden retriever.

In the rain that drives the reflection of the beauty within, we draw near we are right behind him, we are there, he is there with us, in that road we have driven we are side by side as we rode in peace and faith and he drove in fear and craving...

Driving hour after hour in silence
Filed after field song after song

Droning silence of the winded cars
Crack of the window that I hold open
To hear and breathe in the air outside

The hollow hole in my heart in my chest yearning to speak,

sing, yell my truth

From the rooftops I call in my native tongue of tongues who

and where and how am I.

Where do I go from here? Who comes to me in my dreams as I

wake in silence I scream his name, he calls to me in infinity and

risks being revealed to spirited form asunder wonder gratifying

waves that test time in line with natures way, the body's way.

Holy day in spirit time we hold space for one another to

drink the wine that is our truth divine.

Landing in times square you are held in parachute bars

Of justice you, inspire the hard live wire to zing inside my brain

Passing thinking for intuition my left side salutes the wise voice

of angels

It s time to share my talents and gifts.

To serve as the dove amongst stars

In the garden playing the fluted melody of old salute stars

dancing as one

Turning to turn all into slaves of the master warship on high and

spin towards our yearning destiny revealed.

To trust in a world where we do not trust ourselves, our

thoughts

Feeling inner most emotions and inner voices as they tell us

our truths

I do not understand how the two people I have trusted recently

have beamed back I do not trust them…how is that possible-I

have to prove that I trust them

What is the message-to trust myself

Kicked out of the water today for a few hours

Feeling as though I was kicked in the stomach only to recover

to feeling my closed and tired heart of trusting again

What is going on what am I feeling-those triggers those

reaction those projections upon me on me to me

For me

All not for me at all

To live amidst the ruins of my heart is so hard

Live amongst strangers that are quasi family friends community

Takes time to know and build there is no instant I trust you,

except a feeling or intuition to so do. When years come along

with the price tag more is on the line and more can be woven

and has been woven into the fabric of trust-I give 100% trust

until it is taken away.

However long that may be but that is who and how I am.

Taking responsibility for my tones and actions and place I am

holding.

My heart is my heart and its security system is wide and thin and dense and dark full of holed light on the window pane sill, it beckons for all to come and greet to try to break the alarm system, although only few get through and are committed and trusted friends.

For you who are great beings-are human too, and I need to always see that.
As evolved and brilliant as you are, you need to see you as you are-human.

My heart so open to you
Now closed
Doors are locked and security system turned on
The daggers I know so well have been taken out in my hell
Shell of my bed my womb my den I pray once again for healing and light
To shed the fur of my skin that I live in

Naked where I feel everything and everything hurts

From those that trust who do not know what I have given them

and they then throw it away on the street for the dogs to chew.

Those who know how precious my heart is keep it holy and

pure.

Even they may attempt to throw it away but history has shown

itself as they have protected it for so long.

Peace offering in the house, difficult to hold nearing the fruit of

the labor of friendship

Was taking care of your needs by going to shop did not want

eggs in my car to plop.

I went back to my old ways of celibacy when I started dancing. I was miss sexual on the stage and on the floor of the club. I established a routine for the first time since I was in high school. Wake up, take my vitamins, drink some good heathy juice, and go to work. Almost everyday in the beginning, and then drive to work, the strip club. At nine thirty in the morning. If you arrived early, in the top three, you were able to receive a free house fee.

When I started to value the dollar I decided it would be a motivation to arrive early, and keep myself on a schedule of some sort. I tried three days off, four days on. Only weekends. I had to see where my customers were coming from and when they would be there. I also needed down time. Free time with no thoughts or club energy. It drains you, sucks the life energy right out of you, literally sucking your soul life. There were many girls that were sucked in by drugs and worked long hours just to pay off their addictions, or even sold the stuff themselves. I was lucky in that respect.

I was a love addict and so for me at this time in my life, I was able to be free from drama, most of it at least and focus, focus on MONEY. Which was a first for me? I always made just enough to survive. Always wondered why I did not make the big bucks in all of my prowess as a tantrika. I kept it humble and very pure. Like a Mary Magdalene.

If I would have started pole dancing at any age before thirty-five I would not be alive today, that is a fact. The love addiction would have reared its fangs right into my skin and devoured each morsel, very quickly.

My favorite manager at the club said girls got addicted to the money they made in the club, and that was the main reason they stayed. Chad, was on duty certain days and times, and when he was I would get so turned on, as I imagined him watching me at every moment. I would make a ridiculous amount of dollars. **It was hot.**

On his final day at the club, I nearly lost it on stage as they announced his departure, and danced one final dance for him. He was leaving for a sales career, having been a bounty hunter before the club days, and met his fiancé, she was a dancer, who had decided to leave the underground, and he was leaving with her at age 27.

I revealed my lusting for him and all of my money making rewards by thinking he was watching me, he said it made his day, smiled and moved on. It turns out we were lovers in a past life, and I remembered him.

The house I bought had vacancies across the street and all over the neighborhood, foreclosures were everywhere, and I had bought just in time. I had spent two months looking for the right property, location, and narrowed it down eventually. My agent was new, young, and was willing to drive me anywhere to make a buck. This was before I knew the value of a buck myself. However, I did appreciate her time. It was a stressful and emotional process, my intention was to live there until I got married. I was thinking it would maybe take another five years, who knows if ever. So I took some advice from an agent I knew to look for the biggest property in the very best condition, they all looked the same, so it was a hard choice. I finally found one, that met my criteria with some custom stone tile work on the floor in a temple like circular fashion, and then rose bushes in the front walkway. I had felt like this was a sign form the gods that this way my house. I had a special connection with roses and wanted my sanctuary to feel like a temple.

The process on the front and back end of the sale was overwhelming and I was not prepared to withstand all of it alone. Managed, and survived my first night in my new house, sleeping on the floor, waking up to a cold, empty house, on Valentine's Day. How ironic, the house I had been longing for, I now owned, in a neighborhood I would have never lived in had you paid me before in a rental situation, let alone something to buy, yet here I was, my dreams fulfilled, how wonderful. I was out of funds, after buying all the furniture and decorating the house with all the things I needed. I was thrifty, put sheets on the windows at first, and needed to find a job to pay my bills. In the back of my behind, I kept hearing stripper, stripper, this is it, now or never, you have to make a buck to survive this one. I had broken it off with my mother following a conversation I had with her, and meant it this time. No more mommy supporting and controlling me. She had finally given me the money to buy a house, and I was willing to be flat broke and a stripper at this point before I would take any more of her abuse. I was done with being a marionette, living in fear of a master who spewed disdain and hate in the same cocktail she called love.

Her death grip had lost it's hold, as I began to hold and cradle and believe in myself, now that no one could take this house away form me, or kick me out, as I had been kicked out of so many times.

There were sacrifices that had to be made, and many lessons to be learned, Including one about adulthood, responsibility and growing up. I had been the adult, mother, and sex slave since age four, and had some time being child and teen allowing my mother to support me financially for many years. Now her divorce settlement was final, and I was calling it quits.

The house was not haunted, we checked and cleared the energy with a white candle. I caught my hair on fire as I walked around this new house. I felt bold and proud with my young lover by my side, he was helping me out with the handiwork, I was paying him ten dollars an hour. I was so sexually attracted to him, that I had to ask him to just be friends with me, he agreed. He knew how to make me scream, was a firefighter.

He started to pee blood and I thought nothing of it. I did not have anything, it was only after we broke it off that I became sick.

I had no idea how to take care of a house. What had I gotten myself into? I was the one they never let mow the grass, or take out the trash, and yet here I was alone, taking on a foreclosure. Almost move in ready.

It was a nightmare.
One I welcomed.

Everything form hiring something to teach me how to mow the grass to hiring shady electrical handyman who left me with open wiring the day of a lightning thunderstorm, I almost lost my mind again.

After a few months went by, some people moved into the house across the street. I felt a negative energy immediately and was worried but did not know why. They were south of the

Border smuggling people and transporting them into the United States. It was creepy.

More than creepy.

I had cleaning ladies trying to set me up with their divorced with child sons and others trying to redecorate instead of clean. All of it was a nightmare.

I was afraid of being in the house most nights and some days, which certainly defeated the purpose of feeling safe. I was safe in other ways, and had to deal. There were months that went by were I was not afraid, and some I was. I had a convertible with a broken top, which I was swindled into buying, and was furious. Yet again swindled in the car I bought, even when I did have a man by my side I ended up with a car with a broken engine, a broken top, and some I hated.

My white jaguar broke down in Colorado, in the middle of winter, I was broke and drove there to live with a friend of mine, who was about thirty years older than me. He promised me nothing. I met a hot young mechanic talking about my car that died on me, and almost lost my life to carbon monoxide poisoning at a shabby motel I stayed in while deciding what to do with my car.

I know I could have, should have sued the motel and threatened to do so, but by then, I literally had no physical or emotional strength, was alone in the world, broke, a car I had just paid seven thousand dollars cash for, and was swindled out of, had a faulty engine. Bought it from a BMW mechanic who bought it for a small ride during his wedding entrance.

Slapped slapped slapped and slapped again, Hard.

We were in his office at night, and he was leaning over me as I swiveled in his chair, he said, I wonder what my mother would think of raising a Jewish child. Well, I said, it would be Jewish by default, as it would come through my womb, he would not be raised Jewish.

We were destined for each other, I was sure of that if anything, and knew the baby was going to be a very special one, or two or three. Well, not three. Paul mentioned, he wanted three children on our second date, and I said I wanted four dogs, so we compromised on two children and two dogs. We would get one together as I already had Princess.

He liked hunting dogs, as he was a master hunter, luckily as I was a huntress and new how to shoot my bow, I needed a man who was stronger than me according Greg, my biological father. Well, I had not found anyone who met those criteria as of yet, and somehow I felt Paul did just that.

He took control of the conversation from the get go on the first date, and told me he was very aggressive in the bedroom as he cam over to my side of the sushi table, and melted his lips intertwined with the green match ice cream tea ball in my mouth. Sensuous would hardly describe the tingling I felt all over, absolutely everywhere.

I was waiting until a love statement before we headed to the bedroom, but I decided to stop for a little bit in his truck, before he took me back to my car.

I had just sold my house, which I had been waiting for, and had more cash than I had ever had in my life. I was going to celebrate my victory with him. We were going to take a cruise, he was thinking Mexico, I was thinking anywhere with you. I always imagined going anywhere for someone who truly loved me and I them.

One day Paul woke up to his playboy life, sat up in bed, feeling like a different man. He did not know what was changing inside of his mind and body.

He felt a gnawing at the base of his spine, and a blurriness inside of his head. There was no woman by his side. They had all left, even though he could call one up at any hour or place, and have one by his side. He was tired of the meaningless life, loveless sex that was highly overrated and he had being doing it along time. Empty but good.

He felt his heart opening to an expanse he had never felt before. He looked at his palms and rolled on to his side, lingering in his single-dom, and decided right then and there it was time. Time for the sacred sharing. Bringing someone into his world. Trusting someone else with his every thought and whim and desire, fear and passion, vision, and dreams. It was time.

His pad was the same one he bought, with his father's help to his first marriage, but he knew now he was ready to buy another one until he found his true love. This house no longer served him or his new wife to be. Wife. He thought, she would have to be hot, smart, sexy, passionate and holy. She would be his. Only his. Not in a controlling way, well maybe in the bedroom, it would be a mutual intensity. A relationship based in reality that was sacred, raw, hot and holy.

Unbreakable, and unshakeable, for the times of destruction lay ahead of the world. They both would need a solid partner to rely and depend on. "I can trust her when times get tough," he thought. They would move to Montana and start the Bed and breakfast they had talked about, and prepare for doomsday. What would be doomsday for those who do not prepare that is.

I woke up from this dream, and realized it could be happening as most of my dreams were prophetic, not necessarily time wise, but they usually did show up one way or another in reality.

It was time to settle down and have a family, Paul's dream as well. He wanted babies, and he decided to create something meaningful in his life besides his business, to open his heart and share all that he had worked so hard to build. Now who was he going to create this life, this family, this dream with exactly? He was not so sure, and yet was he ever.

Paul called me the night I had lost faith that I was ever going to find someone to love me and settle down and create a family with. Dreams complete with a white picket fence, a garden I could tend everyday, and a few kids and dogs running around.

I was sitting in my hotel room, with all the candles lit up, and the music playing soft electric spiritual echoes of past times, lives, and future fantasies, I was dancing the dance, the last prayer, the last ritual giving up to the gods and angels of the universe to deliver him to me. I want to be swept off my feet, yes, my prince charming on a black horse or a black hummer, does not really matter.

He saw me. I just knew he did. I knew he felt my love with his heart and would remember when the time came.

I had let go and the ball was in his court. He had to step up and come and find me. Propose his vision and profess his love to me.

I was in Paris on a business trip when the call came in.

I was dancing, for him. He must have felt it in the stars alignment with the way he felt that morning when he woke up. His intuition, his knowing of what his heart felt he could not deny any longer, enough was enough. Enough fake women with fake boobs, giggling and smiling, following his every order, enough of the ditzy flighty airheads that fluttered around him. He was ready and this time he was playing for keeps.

I knew that one day his call would come. It could be in a year's time, but damn it I was now ready and did not want to wait that long. I was fuming and adamant that I had done everything to heal and prepare for him and our life together, so why was he dragging his feet to contact me.

I had to surrender.

When someone deeply listens to me, I unfold the petals of the lotus

The womb waiting to be opened, and filled, with ecstasy

With life giving birth, to truth

When I deeply listen to you

I hear your heart longing too reach mine

I hear the whisper of the birds dance

Fly to the heavens

In silent romance, I ask you for a kiss

When you deeply listen to me, you see my soul for more than a moment,

You, become the one, with expert eyes

The one who will not lie

The one who will hold me when I cry

Out to you, when I do not listen deeply to me

When I cry out deeply, when I did not listen to you

You will hear, you will know, you will feel

My womb as it closes and yearns to reopen its petals, again

In my opening, I surrender

In trust, ecstasy is born.

Here it was, game time. It was finally here, His call. My heart stopped beating as I looked at the screen and saw his numbers, I did not even have his phone number anymore.

I took five deep breaths, inhaling and exhaling very slowly, well

I thought, had to be good news, or else he would not be calling.

I listened to his message, deep, soft, clear voice. I wanted to

be his, I wanted his voice to drone over into my deepest

desires of being the only woman he would ever call again with

the intention of making a home with, a life with, a family with,

and many beautiful memories.

Not to mention making the highest form of love with sexually.

Twice a day would be fine if that was what he wanted. My

intention was to always give Paul his personal private love

chamber, infusing him with vitamin M.

I would be the tantric wife.

I was living in New York City in a loft of Lexington Ave. I had a

thriving private practice counseling some of the top attorneys,

and business people in downtown Manhatten, and all over the

world. I was flying here to there, like a busy bee, when the I got hit by a train.

Everyone was in shock. " A *literal* train? your joking," they said. Nope, I was a walking miracle. Some people just did not know how to respond at all and stared at me dumbfounded, they felt the level of the miracle by my presence. The bare essence that spirit had saved me. The manager of the car rental store's father had been a railroad inspector of train accidents for twenty-eight years, and said there were very few people who came out alive.

I had just moved downtown from the investment property, and was living high on the hog. The three months following meeting my love mate, and receiving great grace in my investments brought a great storm before the great light. Just as Paul was brought to me, and then taken, the shiny black Benz was gifted and then taken, but returned better than it's original form.

Somehow I did not move when I heard the bells. Everyone was waving and doing what they could to get me off the tracks. On the tail end of the train tracks, I was blind-sighted by the enormous train that just crashed into my Benz. The rescue fire team, offered their services, I thanked them and waved them away. The officer who approached me demanded to see my license and registration, scolding me with the question, what's your problem," right off the bat. I asked him what his problem was, I had just been hit by a train, and survived, I asked him to have some compassion. The cameras were rolling, I noticed later on, and his tape was as well, it was all of file. They sent another officer to fill in for the good cop. This one, was seeking to control as they all are, but also for some compassion from me, about it being Monday and how the transition had been hard for him all morning long. I think he forgot I just got hit by a driving steel metal train that smashed into my car, and left me standing there, alive able to listen to him. It was a beautiful sight.I thought maybe I was dreaming.

I was alive, did not lose consciousness, and was unharmed, miraculously.

A harsh lesson to learn by the angels and god to wake me up from my unaware slumber, to pay attention at all times to everything and take action.

Opening my the veil that had blinded my eyes before fully opening them wide. To all truth as it truly is.

Black became white. From my toe nail polish to my clothes. I dreamed a black Mercedes and a white Mercedes. The twenty pounds I had gained in toxicity was leaving my body. The clogging of my pores and my life from emotional excess, when I was in fear and felt lack, led me to the a place of hardly being able to walk and seeing more doctors and being on more medications that I have in my whole life put together. The birth control I had feared taking for twenty years, I had the water retention, the moodiness, many things I had feared, it did help my acne. I broke the fear barrier and lost all the weight when I went off the birth control pills, and committed to the next sexual partner being my fiancé,' in a committed loving partnership on every level.

When the positivity came flowing in, the negativity including water and fat came flowing out. Fat cells are the beginnings of cancer. They are the mutation of the emotional body from fat into cancer. The deeply held compacted fat cells morph into the cancer cells that replicate if the emotional and spiritual body is not healed. Repressed resentment will build up and spill over into you like a volcano exploding, with hot lava into your pores and the people around you.

I was at dinner around happy hour time, at a restaurant on the Upper east side, and I man sat down next to me, as I was getting ready to leave. He says I would be the kind of person he would like as a neighbor, someone that would mow his lawn for him, if he was out of town. " I would love to mow your lawn," I said. The bartender, who looks just like Ellen Degeneres, says she has been told she looks like Princess Diana all her life, I have never heard that expression before.

The man seems sweet, Cory`, was his name, and I never did get profession, what I did get was a story, when I asked him if he was gay. He was in Mykonos, with his wife of eleven years, and was hit on by a gay male on a nude beach. The story revolved around the details of an American couple who had plopped themselves right in front of Cory and his wife, and opened legs while she was lying naked on the blanket in front of him. He had a physical arousal response, and was not able to get up and get a drink when his wife asked him to. The naked woman was spotted by his wife, and she was furious at his erection and how he had lied about not watching her.

He was dressed as his wife supposedly did not allow his to disrobe which he desperately wanted to do, she forbade it. He quickly told me she was, "Damaged" Goods," her father had sexually abused her when she was thirteen. I bit my lip until after the story ended. I had laughed out loud at it's absurdity, listened to his pain, disgust and distrust of his ex-wife who betrayed him and with women AS A WHOLE. I suggested it may not be a good idea to describe any woman in the manner he was speaking in, and that maybe he had not healed from the issues from his past marriage. He laughed out loud at the absurdity of my suggestion, as it was twenty-three years ago, and how of course he had healed from it.

The statement Cory had made, was the internal thought reality, torturous, I had been living for thirty-five years, off and on, up and down, working on healing just that experience and those tormenting thoughts. I was ready to hear those words from someone. When I was fully healed and was able to hear the truth of his hurt and resentment, from twenty-three years ago, and most likely many years prior, from his family of origin.

It will show up as disease, eating away at your core. Hiding inside layers of excess of any kind, will feel like temporary protection, a full body mask, skin packed onto skin, false protection from affection, an excuse, a genre for debate, discussion, waging a war within your own body, trying to stay healthy, as you may do anything to keep your subconscious repressed. Memories that no longer serve you, haunt need to be released. Forgiven.

Something about the black handgun Max kept in the closet hidden underneath my mothers clothes, the very ones I would steal to wear when I was eight, made me feel a sense of power, the knowledge of what was hidden, the secrets that lay beneath the closed doors, I was privy and access to. I had to forgive, deeply and completely those who annihilated my soul, attacked my body and my essence for so many years, to heal my self. To give universal and unconditional love.

Ceremonies of forgiveness, rituals, and over a decade of climbing the staircase to send love to those that had betrayed me most. I did in the closet, and shut down to get away from it all. Many times. It was only my grandmothers loving touch and gaze that could rock me out of leaving my body, it she who believed me, that said my words were not lies. A four-year old does not lie about being sexually abused. She saw it on my skin.

Pale, dressed in red. Sacred. Womb. Golden tomb.

There were others who did not believe. Others would scorn my truth. A truth a fought to know. A truth that came from deep within the innards of all timeless records, of akashic recording.

I arrived on her doorstep, fully phobic of dogs. She had the largest german Shepard I had ever seen waiting at the door to greet me standing by her side. She, Nina, a new therapist at age thirty-eight, said it was time for me to get over my fear of dogs, my mother had instilled in me as a child. My mother told me I was allergic to dogs and cats, I was terrified of all dogs, when one day I was over at a family friend's home, and feeling my fear their dog bit down hard, puncturing the skin of my left arm, when I was six years old. I was not allowed to enter the house without her dog, Gremlin standing guard. I was in Boston visiting after some time abroad and of course had nowhere else to go. I pushed through my lifetime fears of dogs and walked through the fire. Gremlin slept at the foot of my bed and would not leave my side, protecting me as Nina destroyed my truth.

She was my mother's best friend, and I trusted her implicitly. I sat down one night in her newly decorated shabby sheik townhouse, and told her the truth of the abuse.

The following week I telephoned Dolores, my mother, from a pay phone in Manhatten, who blasted me for telling Nina lies, as Nina had decided I was lying. I was devastated, and alone on the streets of New York City. Scorned for the truth.

It took thirty-four years of being told my inner truth and knowing was a lie, to know one hundred percent that my true knowing was the only thing that was true.

Sacred.

Coming into the closet to hide the masks, skins, layers of shame, your safe place from long ago, and now coming out of the closet with new clothes on. Shining. With love. Kindness. Respect. For the love you have found for yourself within. That is the path of loving acceptance of all around you.

When you do not listen to the bells ringing the awareness all around you, you may see the gifts and opportunities right before you. I found a twenty dollar bill I found laying on the ground of the store, the day after I got my car back, and another dollar on the ground the next day. Later realizing, the Universal energies were returning the gifts I was grateful for being able to give. It was a somber right after I had moved back into the city, Sunday, and I asked god to help put a smile on my face, somehow. As I approached my car coming out of the grocery store, some called out to me, told me he was not dangerous, and asked me if I was from the ghetto. He continued by reading me his poems on friendship, love, joy, and life. I was tired. I started to remember all I had been through, struggle, extreme suffering, climbing all the mountains alone, and fighting all of my own battles. Shed some tears, he pulled some heart strings. I told him I would never forget him and that moment. He gave me a real hug. One of the most heartfelt hugs I had ever received, in the parking lot of grocery gourmet. I gave him twenty dollars for two poems, and mostly his loving energy he gave me. His kindness of listening and caring, for that brief moment.

The dollar, lying on the floor, came back to me a week after a moment of grace and giving in a second hand store. I was looking for a small stuffed teddy bear for Princess to play with, when a little four year old barefoot girl, with dirty blonde hair comes up, and says, " You dropped one," startled, I said thank you. I had heard her call out to her father, about some pajamas they had. I noticed he had black and purple circles under his eyes, speaking to one of the employees there about a judge and a sentence. We were checking out at the same time, and the little girl was crying because she wanted the pack of plastic horses instead of the big truck, her daddy said, " he did not have another dollar, and they would have to come back with mommy and get the horses another time. " So, I gave the dollar over, and the dad thanked me. I said, it's for the girl." and he raised her up high to thank me in his arms, her smiled beamed so far and wide, and lit up my heart like nothing else had in months, maybe years. Tears streamed down my cheeks, as I remembered asking myself earlier why I am still going to second hand stores such as this when I am able to afford anything I want now?

Now I knew exactly why I had been called to come there. The cashier told me how earlier that day she had sent a prayer up to god, asking her to bring some solace and peace , some joy to her life. There was a woman who gave another lady behind her in line a twenty dollar bill to help her buy some pants, and that woman in turn, turned around helped the man behind her buy something else he needed and could not afford. It was the angels coming into grace of gifting, giving, and gratitude. The first i had ever given a donation in a church, was ten dollars, and the pastor said it would come back to me a hundred fold. I believed it with all my heart, and the next week my investment property sold.

I made space for the intangible, the impossible, I began to realize I never had real true faith god, the energies of the universe, would bring me someone who I liked. Not someone I did not care for at all. My life was changing.

I was the sacrificial lamb, as was the lamb that Jesus held. As green Buddha held.

Ironically as I was keeled over vomiting over the toilet, I felt all the pieces coming together, I was been shown how my whole life was a master spirit walk quest to teach me true grace, humility, god. From arrogance to false humility to true humility. Everything began to change. The way I dressed, no longer the shiny high priced hooker look, but the lady look from years past, during those seven years of remembering purity and throwing wearing my inside on my outside again. My new dentist did not recognize me. He was shocked when I reminded him about a conversation we had had just a week prior, when I first stopped into the office. His face became very red.

I put away the flashy Japanese kimono, peach satin with black lace robes, that were hanging on my bed post, they were such a beautiful decoration, reminding me of my beauty, and everyone on the street outside the loft for the matter.

My building had all glass windows, and everyone at the Federal building got a great show, or thought they did, including the workers down below. Getting a glimpse of what they hoped they would see if they waited long enough. In the first few months I had many familiar cars driving by, waiting on the side streets until I would come out and play for them. Of course, I never did, I know, I'm not any fun am I? I placed everything inside of drawers that was making its home on all of my countertops. I unclogged, and uncleared absolutely everything. I had been doing this for fifteen years, cutting and clearing that is, until my eyes were finally able to see. I sat back on my couch laughing out loud at the absurdity of how many planting pots I had, trying to keep the plants alive in my city loft, repotting and planting all of them, until I finally realized I really wanted a garden in the country to work on everyday. Now, I really only wanted and needed exactly the amount I already had. That was the way it was with so many things I had, which was relatively minimalistic.

Belinda, I met a woman on the street, dressed in my lady like clothes, who was telling me about a time she went shopping for baby clothes on an endless budget, in Aspen, and how the store clerk ignored her, and took care of the woman dressed like a "hooker." So I asked her what the hooker look alike was wearing, and she said, " An ill fitted shirt and, leggings, and spiked heels, 'but she had a lot of money," she said. It was good to know she thought I was a dressed like a lady, a confirmation there as she kept talking to me on the corner of Park Avenue.

She had just "bulk shopped" as her twelve year old daughter described it. Her mother had admitted to being a shop-a holic in conversation who turned her desires around, and became a rep for people selling their ware online. After spending $150,000 on In Vitro fertilization to produce the child of their dreams, her endless budget ended in divorce. She told the sales, clerk, who implied she did not have enough to buy a hundred dollar dress, that she was already one hundred and fifty-thousand dollars into the baby already, so she could probably add another hundred to the tab.

Belinda was someone who knew her creativity was being squelched by the prescription drugs she was taking. She wanted the diagnosis so she could affirm to herself she needed to fit into society, and be normal. In essence, her creative voice was the soul voice being repressed again. I could see a deeply spiritually attuned being in her eyes, she understand that god was the energies of the universe coming together to form create and destroy.   Transmission, a reintegration, a reincarnation.

Of a Temple Cat from Egypt, an enlightened being, guarding the temple and the Queen. My dog, Princess. Even she got sick. Animals very closely aligned and attuned to your energy body will take on your illness into their bodies to help you heal. I then prayed to the gods to help me digest my change, to the middle of the road to lady like status. Returning.

The Vet and techs said she was the bravest Chihuahua they had ever seen. Her rump had an abscess, she took on my illness, and helped transform my integration and acceptance of my new life.

The beginning of a new day. It was the storm before the greatest light, the love of my life.

His message laid it all out there on the table.

He missed me and wanted to have dinner the next night.

Thankfully, it was the night after, as I could hardly contain the wiggling excitement building in my chest, my holy of holies, my heart.

How could I, after waiting, yearning for a lifetime, be reunited after I let go of my love mate?

Well, dinner it would be, and of course I would go.

If you let something go, and it comes back to you, it was meant to be they say. I believe it.

Deepening the golden edge of time
Blowing winds kiss, the ends of eternities gaze

Inside of the womb mist
Glittering, glowing, internalizing the story
Devotional hymns
Determined Glory of sunshine blazing through the drowning
Cornish hens cluck

Rhythmic interventions sounding at dawn

The seagulls call us down to the docks edge where

You and I meet

Intertwined at our souls core

We stand at the confluence

Awaiting Resurrection.

Holding love.

When love has to wait at the door

For the handle to turn

Before the key has been placed in the groves

Before he returns

You hold the door cracked

Open

In your arms

Holding

The Golden Key

I walked into the arms of my beloved. He flew to meet me in Paris the next night. It was winter, white sky, snow lay upon the streets, above the clouds inside of the trees, a blanket of purity, freshness, newness, of a lifetime, about to unfold, and wrap its magical wings around us both. In its womb Paris held us, as we held each other. Paul met me at the elegant Parisienne Chateau de Eiffel Bistro on the balcony, at the top of the Eiffel tower. Standing in the most romantic city in the world, with the love of my life, Paul professed his love for me right then and there, as he inscribed Je t'aime, I love you, into the metal railing.

He did not waste any time, stared into my eyes, and touched my heart. He pulled out a small black box, and said, I know you are the one. The one I love, The one I want to spend the rest of my days with. I promise to be faithful and love and protect, you be honest, and cherish you always.

I was lost in his eyes, his touch, but oh, so found.

In Paris, overlooking the city lights my dream became a reality.

Never give up on your dreams.

Setting the stage for bursting forth
Bringing forth from wombscapes.

Eyelids live in allowing all to be settled in mayhem,
Allowing the flow to turn into the weaver gold web bundle
Of massive turnabout
Lives from the past for
The unveiling has begun

Quan Yen's heart so peaceful, eyes lowered in humility,

*Set forth in solitude, solid ground foundation beneath her shoe step
into freedom*

*Standing proud as she acknowledges her beauty admiring the mirrors
That have been laid out for her gaze,*

Inside the Labyrinth *walls, the egg shell breaks open to the expansion
contraction*

*The tree of life shattering into infinitesimal broken vessels we are to
face as illusion*

*Breaking free of our masks that guard our hearts and tame our
destines
Carved out lines molding into a subterfuge of linen tablecloths that
lie face down on pillows Softness to rest medicine.*

*Profundity masters the realms we dive into on whimsical nights of
past*

*Hollows out Carbondale feelings, wet in delving into the thickness of
scalp*

That unites kings and queens as common men

*Coercing mortal creatures in trivial pursuit of legends lost that are
found and within our loins tale of despair*

The love, prophecies for-tell of coming days..

*Sensuous tales of master doom come in lines of fairies bloom
Indiscretion many have told the pathways to karma-*

*Land fly with the birds of nested wing trip patterned males of ripened
fruit vines*

Calendula *stops the blood flow of worlds, merging shedding blood ties,*

Baths of healing and purity sing stellar bluebird song

Mystical shaman tune from long ago....into misty fire pits smoldering waves

Calming peaceful minds in a slumber, waking momentous breaths of joy

No need for negativity-

Knowing when to share saga dreams with spirit

Sage passionate artist visions

THAT HOLD GRACE

IN THE PLACE OF SPADES THE QUEEN LINES THE WALLS THAT HIDE BEHIND ILLUSION

STANDING AT THE FOUNTAIN OF YOUTH
YOU JOIN IN SILENCE

THE STONE EDGE WEDGE OF WEAVING WORLD
PASSAGE OF TIME

INSIDE YOUR HEAD IN YOUR WORLD
I DREAM YOUR DREAM AND SEE WITH YOUR EYES

AS MY HEART TONIGHT IN YOUR DREAMS
THAT BECOME MINE

TONIGHT.
I SEE THE MOON AS YOURS AS MINE

IN MY LIFETIME THE STARS LIGHT
MY EYES AS JEWELS WORN LIFETIMES PAST

IN YOUR HEART LIGHTS THE FIRE OF
ANCIENT WHISTLE TUNES YOU NOW REMEMBER

WE ARE HERE TO REMEMBER AND JOIN THE DANCE HOWLING
LIKE SOUL LOVERS MAGIC SPRINKLED OVER SHORES OF THE
DEAD

BRINGING TOGETHER BODIES AND SOULS
BRINGING THE BODY HOME TO LIVE
IN ITS SANCTUARY

PERSPIRING

Perspiring, dripping wet with emotion
Feel your skin brushing against cheek bones
Smelling pheromones oozing out of pores
 Breathing all in

Body building pain assessment
Weaver of lives crossing paths
With one another yearning for connective care

Seeking stunning blueness gold silver lake of eyes
Massaging my lips quivering underneath the moonlight

Only to be known by You
 Past stories have become old.

Disappearing into smoke ravishing
Todays flames
Reminding us of a mortality

Tonight gaze whispers beyond the fire.

Always remain calm

Like the sea water

Boundless Light

Opening the heart as wide -breaking the walls of diffusive barriers
Unwind the strip mall bows and bends to bow out of confusion
Falling into abyss with mind intact-infusion
 Energetic source boundless light attracts love is you
Melting into the flow of creation divination of breath and moments
Crowning down spine

Letting go-releasing into the void-allowing for radical acceptance
Tingle waves of structure

Breaking melting into fuse light
Coming back to the depth of true reality
What is -now

Embracing what was-understanding acknowledging and moving on
To hold self as love as us world you mom you dad
Holy brothers and you holy sisters
In my mouth tastes bittersweet melodies of long ago ancient wisdom
Held wanting to be explored

Not needing approval or attention from you, me-
From him or her
Mirror images fade collide and come
Face to face with thoughts that show you yourself
Take away the desire for love, approval, and appreciation
Be with what is.

Love Surrounds

Underneath the shimmery night
The stars shine bright and let us know that we are not alone
Love does surround us- and makes us who we are in every fiber of our
being
Life makes sense on the logical plane
Although some live from an emotional center
The world turns on the axis of past and future even though we must
be here now
We must honor and protect ourselves for that is really all we have
We are one and the same
Sometimes we must part to rejoin
To cherish our most intimate place

To heal from the terror that was and is

Not to hide behind closed doors that were always open for all to see
For all to hear and laugh and smile
For all who knew and denied
The atrocities to difficult to bear

To stand by and watch as children have none to eat
Where to sleep

To take care of oneself is to take care of one another
To understand that without ourselves we cannot do so
To understand that one can never fully be in another's shoes
No one can judge just guard and honor-look back and see how
We are here today-what made us weak and strong

What a miracle our existence is.

www.ingramcontent.com/pod-product-compliance
Lightning Source LLC
Chambersburg PA
CBHW070015100426
42740CB00013B/2502